Herman's Sister

Ramendeep Dhoot

Clink
Street

Published by Clink Street Publishing 2022

ISBN:
978-1-914498-78-7 - paperback
978-1-914498-79-4 - ebook

In thanksgiving to God, who gave me the strength to write and created my book

This book is inspired by and written for, my beloved brother Herman. I hope it makes you proud. I love you more than you can imagine. 'Together Forever.' 'See you soon.' xxx♥

Dedicated to my wonderful and amazing mum, Baljinder Kaur Dhoot, who is an incredible silent hero, a phenomenal mother and a remarkable woman in her own right.

Thank you to my extended family and friends in the UK and India for being there when my world collapsed

A special mention is given to those friends and angels on earth who have stood by my side through the darkest of moments, not just at the time of my recent unbearable pain, but months and years after the event, when the ache lingers in my soul and the shadow of grief stays by my side.

Thank you Helen Tavares, Sam Ahmed, Neelam Chima, Rashda Ali, Holly Ann Luton Jackie D Gayle, Marissa Harvey, John Bowen, Jagjit Mankoo, Katherine, Claire Chambers and Dr T. Thank you for truly being there and hearing my heart, especially when I felt so alone.

Thank you to CRY (Cardiac Risk Young), Samaritans, Cruse Breavement, Think Aorta, Care for the Families and The Compassionate Friends. I don't know how I would've coped with you.

Thank you to you - my reader. Thank you for taking the time to read my book. I hope it touches your soul.

Introduction

Welcome to my world. To my story. I hope it connects with you in some way. I've kept a journal for more than two decades. Battling my way through life, my journal was a way of capturing, reflecting and measuring how far I'd come whilst trying to find a place of gratitude. After navigating a dysfunctional childhood, with a backdrop of domestic violence, bullying, failure, rejection, mental health issues, parental grief, and so much more, I thought my life was now on track to get better, because, as they say nothing stays the same. Life changed, got better and I was happy. Now was my time. Our time, to live a happy normal life, with the people I loved most in this world – my wonderful mum and beloved brother. We would always describe ourselves as 'one heart', with each of us making the shape of a full heart. We would say how we couldn't live without each other. Together we had endured and overcome so many trials and tribulations in this life, that our love was unyielding as ever. On a separate note, I was in love and looking forward to building a future with a man I once adored. Life was good.

Then, at age 40, when I thought I'd be happily married with a few kids running around, I found myself single. I thought he was the one and this love would open the doors to all the happiness I'd ever craved. It didn't happen. Finding myself, a British Indian woman single at 40 jolted me into a half eye open rude awakening to the reality of my life. Fuck.

Well, that was all a drop in the ocean, compared to the tsunami that was about to erupt in my life in 2019. At 2:17pm on Wednesday 9th Jan 2019, my best friend, my heartbeat, my world, my brother was declared deceased. Just like that. A dark, heavy cloud suddenly overshadowed my life. A life I once knew and lived in parallel with was over. Just like that. Suddenly. My life dramatically changed, when I was catapulted into a world of sudden unimaginable and unbearable grief. There was no notice, no time to think and no time to prepare (if you ever can prepare for such an event).

I have experienced bereavement before, but this grief was something else. Unfathomable. A new kind of pain, with a distinct aura, sensation and one that would forever transform me and my existence from that point on. An experience that would change the core of my being and and my future life experiences. A moment of forced adjustment. I had no choice. There was nothing I could do. I had to just take the bullets life was firing at me and those I love.

Sudden grief arrives in the form of an unexpected visitor that catapults you from a safe place to a world of utter despair. You're forever changed and feel like you're floating between two different worlds – your new reality which seems unreal and the old life you crave back. You still cannot fathom what has happened and how your life has changed, just like that. You're left with an invisible scar, that no-one can see, yet it's always there. Like a new shadow. A new friend. Only you can see. Only you can feel. A constant ache in all that you do. It's never-ending. Life is never the same. You lose yourself and reflect on who you once were, before the tragedy. No experience feels like it should do anymore. The taste of life becomes bland and bitter. It had for me. Like a light had been turned off and a heart once warm and compassionate was now hard and numb.

So, here I am. A British Asian woman in her 40s, never married, no kids, no nieces or nephews, no siblings (in the physical form – I'll come onto that later) and one parent. All my friends are either with a partner, married or have families. Or they have one of the above. I was left empty of any male presence in my life and void of a future I could not yet see or imagine. My father, brother and partner gone. The end of a relationship is incredibly painful too, but mine was dwarfed by my grief.

My family once consisted of a full house: both my parents, me and my brother and my nan. Now there's just 2. However, I'm still here. By the grace of god, I have something to give. To share and I believe it is my story. It is this book. I do very much believe we all have a purpose in this world. If it connects with you and helps you in anyway, then I have fulfilled that purpose. My life has been bitterly cruel, yet I carry hope and light that things will get better.

I want to share my story. To share my experience of life so far, that I believe, many of you will be able to relate to – perhaps a particular topic may touch you, as opposed to the full juggernaut of drama in my life. I want to connect with you, who pushes through everyday, despite all your obstacles. I want to shine light on the ordinary people of this world who go through daily life battles, without anyone knowing. I also want to acknowledge the millions of talented people who couldn't fulfill their potential. To share it so you don't feel alone. Everyone is trying to do the everyday well. We don't have to 'have it all' – the social media 'likes', the perfect family, the money, the body, the looks. It seems to be a way of life, almost everywhere. Today's existence seems to be lived for others to validate, full of comparisons and others expectations on how you should be living your life. We all have a story - it's our footprint in the world. One that is unique to us. Share your scars. It will help us all heal. Share and navigate the human experience. We all know the power of being vulnerable with each other. It creates a deeper connection that feels familiar. We all experience the same emotions through different life lenses, at different times. I see on social media, people are losing themselves in the midst of 'how life should be'. How they should look. What kind of life they should be living. The uniqueness of our individualism seems to be fading away. I will not follow the masses. Challenge. Be curious. Why are things the way they are? Ask questions. Lots of them. About everything. Question everything. Change and reimagine the very fabric of your life. We don't all have to have the same life trajectory. The framework of our current experience of living can be dismantled. Re-construct a new reality. Your reality. Live differently. Do things in a different order. Shake things up. Life doesn't have to be the way you or other people think it should be: school – college/uni – married – kids – work – retire – die. Find new perspectives. My life has forced me to live differently. I guess I wanted to follow the 'right way' but now realise actually there is no right way. There is not order. Only one that is self-imposed, dictated and conditioned by society.

This book is also written to acknowledge you - the silent heroes. I don't claim to have any magic answers or be an expert. This is my story. My qualification for saying what I say, is my experience. Grief and pain is universal our responses to it are individually unique. Personally, I do not follow any 'stages of grief'. It's not a clinical process, that has a start and end. It's ever present. You have to tolerate the intolerable. Walk with a new shadow. I feel transformed at a cellular level. Reconstructing a new me, in a new, unknown world. Starting life again. A life I didn't chose but have to live with. Eventually you learn to endure the pain and embrace the situation, knowing the one you love never really left you as you feel their presence throughout life, as I do. But I'm a firm believer that if one has not lived the specific experience, they cannot even begin to comprehend what it feels like, I don't care how much studying has been done on the topic.

If I can change or influence one life, for the better, or make you think differently, see life differently, give hope then I'd consider that a success.

Truth is I'll never truly be healed from the most recent life event, but I put one step in front of the other and keep pushing through the pain. Time may make the pain a bit lighter to carry, but it will never erase it. I'm not going to say I went through tragedy and now I'm great and have 'recovered'. No. That's not how it goes. It goes like this: Each day you wake up, you force yourself to do something, find an anchor to latch onto, before before the anguish takes hold of you again. Then, there are times where you feel so incredibly rotten and awful, you don't have the energy or motivation to do anything and you stay in bed, paralysed by the thoughts and flashbacks of what the hell just happened or whatever maybe going on in your life.

This is my version of life. I have experienced and continue to experience the statements below. Maybe you can relate one or more.

You feel like giving up on life when you simply cannot take anymore of what it has to offer, no matter how much you try and change your fate. But then I think what if I don't give up? What would be on the other side of this darkness? There will be light some day. Maybe not the same way but nothing stays the same forever.

Feel exhausted from life and want to give up

Cry to sleep at night

Pray and have faith that things will change. I keep praying and believing. Nothing stays the same forever.

Live in fear of the future, I try and remain present

Want to go to sleep and not wake up. I've been here so many times.

Grief. An emptiness. A void that can never be filled. A life forever changed. I am so sensitive to your pain. I know that you and I are not alone.

Sacrifices your own happiness and time to care for someone you love

Work day and night to make ends meet, to put food on the table, to feed their children. My mum did the same.

Appears to 'have it all' on the outside but are hurting inside.

Faking a smile behind a broken heart

Feel alone or have no-one to talk to

Dreamed of being married and having children. I don't give up.

Feel like you're 'left behind' in life. There is no order. That's what makes each one of us unique. Life would be so boring if we all had the same story, the same way at the same time.

Gave my all – my heart, time, energy to someone I loved so very, very much and it didn't work out – My heart broke too. Badly. One thing I know for sure, you can unlove the once loved, with time.

Continue to do the right thing, be a good person, kind, compassionate but yet you continue to suffer. It's ok to be angry, mad at the world. It's ok. I won't quit and be angry forever.

Have more questions about life than answers – I'll continue to question life. Push society's barriers and reframe the current life structure.

When I feel the above, I also know the below:

'This too shall pass....'

'They wondered how could she survive, all the things life had done to her, until they got to know her, then they realized her beautiful angel wings, that looked so soft and delicate, from a distance, were made of steel.'

Reggie Nulan

Early Years: Love and Dysfunction

My mother saw my father on the day they got married. Not a single moment before. They were worlds apart in terms of their match and compatibility. Mum, university educated, a Punjabi language teacher. Dad, with limited education but was in England – the promised land. My grandparents thought mum would have a better life in England. However, nothing could be further from the truth. Mum loved her early years in India. Her father was in the Indian Army, she learnt discipline, hard work, selflessness and enjoyed one of her favourite things – fashion. She often tells me how her father would send her silk from Japan and she'd get beautiful clothes stitched in India. I see in photographs and family tell me how stunning my mum was in her youth. Pure elegance and natural beauty. She enjoyed her youth and her life before she got married. A free spirit, embracing her youth and living every moment. She's still beautiful physically, but what makes her even more gorgeous is her heart. Her kindness, sensitivity, humility, grace, affection and ability to love. I love that about her. To this day, my mother's heart is still in India. It's where she experienced her best life, as I'm constantly reminded.

In December 1976, my beautiful big brother Herman arrived into the world. A glorious day for all. Celebrations and Indian sweets shared amongst family. Mum had given birth all alone, without her husband by her side. Like so many women, all over the world, I know this to be true, even now. Gosh, what must that moment be like? To not have anyone familiar around? To be in hospital, in labour on your own? I'm sure that the arrival of your baby makes up for it all once the delivery and pain subsides. Eventually, I believe my father came to the hospital and was ecstatic to have a son. A son he absolutely adored and doted on from day one.

Twelve months later, I arrived. Mum and my grandparents were delighted that our family was now 'complete'. Mum was desperate for a daughter and was naturally elated. From there on, we shared a bond that to this day feels like one soul in two bodies. I must have done something right to be given the most amazing, wonderful mother that I have. Everyday I'm grateful for her.

Our parents did their best. They did what they knew at the time. Looking back it was a dysfunctional upbringing, with undiagnosed mental health problems, domestic violence and love all amalgamated into one. However, I have accepted that when you know better, you do better. My parents did what they knew was best, at the time. On reflection, my brother and I said our lives would have been very different had we been brought up by just our mother. This is not to say we didn't love our father. We did of course. He's our dad and we love him. But he had issues that no one acknowledged or dealt with. So, it was left to mum. Forty years ago mental health was never talked about. Now with hindsight, I know this played a critical role in the way that my dad behaved, which then had an impact on my brother and me.

I love both my parents. However, as individuals they couldn't have been any different. Worlds apart. They had nothing in common. Mum, a quiet, shy and reserved lady. Very graceful in her mannerisms. Dad, very vocal, aggressive with a raw honesty that people at the time didn't like. He was very simple in his living. Didn't drive. Walked to most places or took the bus. Mum is polite and respectful. Dad was often rude and brutal in his communication style. I remember him telling relatives to leave the house, because it was getting dark. At the time it was considered rude, but I now see his direct approach stemmed from a place of good intention and safety. He just didn't know how to be polite, but his heart was in the right place. His way of expressing love wasn't mainstream in any way.

Our younger years were a blend of love and dysfunction, so it's only natural one of us would be affected more by these opposing upbringing styles.

Primary school was a very enjoyable time in my life. Having that carefree spirit and experience, without any serious hormonal or life stresses was wonderful. I sometimes mentally transport to those years of wonderment and reminisce the playful times. Why can't life just stay like that? Growing up is just too much hard work, for me anyway. The simplicity of those early years can be transformational. I guess we can learn to just be free and happy through whatever challenges life brings us. Easy said than done for sure. Those were probably some of the best of my early years. I was happy, playful and had a pleasant group of friends.

I remember Saturdays were dedicated to a marathon of three Indian films and indulging in Bombay mix. I loved the romanticised storylines and songs. It gave me a deeper sense of love and I really felt like my love life was going to be like an Indian film. I would immerse myself in Indian songs, dreaming of my wedding and handsome husband. It was one of my earliest desires – to be happily married with kids.

During the early 90s, I moved to secondary school, which was a little less enjoyable. I was very nervous and shy. A lot of my primary school friends had gone to other secondary schools. So, I was feeling quite scared about what was to come. During those teenage years, a lot of dysfunction took place at home, with large doses of teenage hormones, which would be too much for any parent alone. So, with undiagnosed mental health, aggression, and an uncompatible marriage, much of the fall out and impact of such chaos would land on the children. There was no intervention because there was no acknowledgement of any mental health issues. When I was around 14, I started to feel connected to people who had overcome struggles and adversity. I'd rush home from school, to watch the *Oprah Winfrey Show*, on terrestrial Channel 4. She has been one of my biggest inspirations. From this, I learnt when you're in pain, you can connect more to and relate to those experiencing the same suffering. I was beginning to understand I was an empath by nature and had a high degree of emotional intelligence. I was able to 'tune into' others pain and emotion.

Unfortunately, as home life continued to deteriorate, my brother bore most of the impact, during his crucial developmental years. He craved that male role model, which unfortunately he didn't find. My father loved Herman very, very much, more so than me. However, the disciplinarian, which is what we needed, wasn't there. My brother searched for this father figure that our father, unintentionally, couldn't be.

Herman. My only brother. Only sibling. A gifted child, known to be exceptionally bright, always drew attention from teachers and pupils. I was always known as Herman's sister, which made me feel so proud because he was popular and so clever and so handsome. They called him 'brainbox'. A natural, raw talent. He was a little naughty too. Once, I remember a primary school teacher placed his desk alone by the sink, where it was dirty and made him stay there for several weeks, as a form of punishment. He was a child that had misbehaved but the response was disproportionate. That experience stayed with him. It created feelings of isolation, rejection and unfairness. Some experiences never leave us. As we grew, I understood that my brother and I were sensitive children. So, early experiences left a long-lasting effect on us both.

I've learnt, when someone does something that is wrong in our eyes, it's important to look beyond what you see or experience. Especially for those with mental health problems or those who've had a 'damaging' childhood or a life event. I've seen so many relationships crumble because the person who's been wronged never attempted to understand why the argument or 'fight' happened. My experience is to always look deeper. Why is someone the way they are? Understand their 'world'. I've practiced this and will continue to, without allowing my ego to get in the way of my understanding, which people I know have done because they fail to see outside their 'own world'.

'We don't see things as they are. We see them as we are'

Mum's faith in god has always been strong. Ever since she was a child, she's been a believer. Then over time, it was only natural when life took a turn for the worst, that her faith was shaken. It was during those difficult times at home, in a marriage with someone she was far from compatible with and then the inevitable impact on her children that she questioned where her god was? Herman became more withdrawn from the world and I became more angry, yet resilient. Mum continued to pray. Eventually, those prayers were answered and we reached a point of 'normality'. Love and peace were restored in our home.

As a teacher, mum was a big believer in education, whilst dad was not. This opposed thinking played out at home. For me, as an adult reflecting now, I feel at this point, Herman's wings were slowly being clipped, especially in his teenage years. As my brother searched for and pursued our father's guidance, the further he withdrew from education. Teachers were very aware of Herman's raw ability and talent. I remember trying to encourage him to study, as his potential was so huge. However, the home environment is where the seeds of raw ability will either flourish or wither. Unfortunately for him, my brother withered and withdrew from the world as an adult.

A natural talent, he did gain straight As at GCSE and was predicted As for his A-levels – Maths, Physics, Chemistry and Biology. I remember letters arriving from the UKs top and most prestigious universities, with conditional offers for Herman to take a place. It felt like something extraordinary, when you're from a working-class background, from immigrant parents to then have golden opportunities coming through your door, without having to pay for any privileges. It was momentary. Herman chose not to go ahead with university. He instead moved to London, to explore life. I do sometimes wonder how my dad's life would have been different , had his mental health been diagnosed in his childhood. I'm sure under all the layers of his personality, there was talent.

Meanwhile, I took the traditional route and went to university. It was a place I came into my own a little. When I initially went, I was overweight. When I left, I had lost weight, gained confidence and felt beautiful. I was becoming my own person. My friends at university would always say that I would be the first to get married, because I was such a 'good family girl'. Never in a million years did I ever think for a second that I, the girl who always wanted love marriage and children so much, would be single in her 40s.

My beautiful mother is and always has been my one constant. More so for me than my brother because, he was more influenced by my dad, which had more of a detrimental effect. Whenever dad would be horrible, mum would bring me roses. She brought colour and light to erase every darkness in my life. God blessed me with the most wonderful mother. Without her, I would not be here. That's for sure.

Mum used to work endless hours, to compensate for dad not working. I remember lifting the net curtains in the front room, at home waiting for mum's car to arrive. She would often come home late, to avoid any drama at home. Every time she was late, I kept thinking something bad had happened to her because Dad would often scare us and say 'She's had a car accident' or 'She's died.' He never realised the impact of his words. This heightened level of anxiety has become a thread throughout my life. Past experiences have put me in a constant state of alarm and a heightened sense of alertness to danger.. There have been countless occasions when mum, who is a type 2 diabetic and had hypos, couldn't speak, her jaw would be clenched and I'd fear the worst. I recall one time in London when I thought she'd gone to the toilet and never came out. I started panicking, thinking she was locked in the toilet and had fainted. I'm always on high alert with her. This fight or flight response accelerated me to new heights after our lives changed forever, in 2019.

Whilst our early years do define us and shape who we become, there are millions who become and remain the very definition that others, place on them. I didn't let that happen. I didn't let someone else define me, until I came into my own. In my early years, I did. I started to believe that I was all the horrible things people had said about me – dumb, thick, slow, daydreamer, etc. I felt like they had moulded me into their definition and I let it set. At the time I didn't understand myself enough to know I am worthy and wonderful. These days I'm in awe of myself! It wasn't until I smashed that mould myself, that I could finally be me – intelligent, articulate, beautiful, kind, loving and so much more. One of my friends said to me 'There are people who are not intelligent and pretend like they are. You are the opposite – you are intelligent but you act like you're not.' This was because I was holding onto and carrying the impression of what others had placed and projected on me. This struck me because, it was not something I was conscious about. It was the beliefs that everyone else had of me that I absorbed.

Now I observe. Not absorb.

Journal:

Sept 15th 2004 – 17:25hrs. Arrived home after uni to find out my dad had passed away. I'm in complete and total shock. He went to sleep and didn't wake up. How does that just happen?

Sept 24th 2004: My dad's service. I've been dreading this day…
   Went into the bathroom and had a panic attack. I broke into a cold sweat.

This was the week that changed the way I viewed the world. I started living in the present moment, making every moment count, because you don't know what's around the corner.

22nd December 2005 – my birthday
I woke up to cuddles from mum, my brother and nan. Unknown to me, during the night, Hermy had decorated a photo of me with glitter and stars, decorated my cake, put banners up!

Later, her came into my room with my present. A white fluffy cardigan and a photo of Jesus. It was all wrapped up! I loved it! Thanks Hermy xx

Wednesday 4th May 2009
Today I wasn't feeling well at all. Been in bed most of the day. My brother Herman has such a kind open heart. He nursed me. Brought me a new hot water bottle and went to town, and brought some cakes from Greggs, which I was craving. We then both sat in the front room and ate them.

Sunday 19th July 2009
Earlier, me and my brother sat in the front room together and talked about life and death. We talked about our funerals. He wants to be cremated. Doesn't want many people to see him. It's difficult for me to hear him talk like this, but I also want to fulfil his wishes. He wants a reading from the Bible. He wants to be closer to God and at peace.

I said I wanted lots of colourful flowers, to which he smiled and nodded.

I'm grateful that I can talk to my brother about anything and he can be so open about his feelings too.

November 2009
Hermy came to watch Micharl Jackson's This Is It with me for the THIRD time!! He knows how Michael Jackson mad I am!!

Wednesday 10th August 2011
Hermy and I had a fight. It always upsets me when we fall out. Later, I'm grateful that we made up. We both apologised to each other and discussed our forthcoming holiday. That's what siblings do. We don't leave it too long, I'm glad.

In our younger years, Hermy and I fought a lot. During our childhood, it was mum who always got our relationship back on track. She was the bridge of love that we crossed during those difficult times. Then as adults, our love grew to a point, that no matter what happened between us or how much we fought, we always had to speak to one another because we simply couldn't be angry for too long. So, I don't understand how some siblings never speak to each other again or lose that relationship, which to me is so sacred. Personally, I also understood that some of his anger towards me was not his fault. I strongly believe that behind all anger is pain. There is no doubt that he was wounded by not being able to fulfil his incredible potential. This lead to depression and a deterioration in his mental health. Our anger was always and eventually diminished by the power of love and open hearts. As a result, we enjoyed some amazing moments together.

12th Feb 2012
Hermy became ill with a temperature and had to go to hospital.

13th Feb 2012
Awww……the house feels empty without H

14th Feb 2012
Hermy self-discharged himself because he wanted to be home with us on Valentine's Day! I spoke with the doctor at the time, who wanted him to stay. He told me how much he respected me. He told me I was a little hero.
*   Hermy came home with us after getting a Valentine's Day card for us!*

23rd April 2012
Hermy called and asked to see me for a few minutes, I went. Awww… it was the sweetest moment. He only wanted to go out and get some fresh air. We walked around the park, sat on some benches. He then pulled a flower out of the tree for me. Aww… I was flooded with love from my brother. I love you.

Thank you for the daily smiles, cuddles and love my dear brother gives. It's magical to see the change in him. This is him. A kind, sensitive and gentle human.

Sunday 22nd March 2014
In the depths of my thoughts, I turned to Hermy and asked 'Where will I find you, when you die?' No reason. I just asked. The question triggered deep emotion. He looked at me with a sad face, almost teary. I melted too and we both had a little cry. Whilst it was initially heart-breaking, it was good and healthy to share the emotion and understand the love we have for each other, as brother and sister.
    Later, he told me I would find him in the stars.

Sunday 21st April 2015
Hermy came over and brought me a Mr Kipling's cake. Such a sweet gesture. We both love cake. I shared my pain of feeling hopeless. He wrapped his arms around me and told me he'll always be here for me. I'm his only sister and he's my only brother. xxx

22nd Dec 2016
My birthday. Feeling a bit grumpy. Mum and Hermy soon extinguished that mood, by singing me a cute Happy Birthday song! Thank you x
    I said to Herman, thanks for being a great brother. He said I'm great cos you're great. Awww…

15th Sept 2017
It's 13 years since dad gained his angel wings.
    Later that evening, Hermy and I spent some quality time together and had a heart to heart. Spoke about life and school. He told me to just be happy. To feel it inside and smile. We talked about family, the past, teachers and our childhood. It felt like an incredibly special moment. We then played some 'brain games' together. He always won, as usual.

18th Dec 2018
Sitting with my brother, in his room. I looked up at the
tree outside his window and said Hermy look at that tree.
Right now, it's bare and cold. Over the coming seasons it will
change, grow and become green. That's how life is. Every
season brings its own colours and textures in our lives. He
looked at me and smiled.

Reading through old journals now brings me immense comfort, because I captured some of the simplest of everyday moments with those I love the most.

Chasing love

The more I craved love, the further it went from me.

Being married and having children is and always has been a dream of mine. It was always something I wanted from my life. The hopeless romantic in me was created by watching endless Bollywood films. Every Saturday, we would watch at least two or three Hindi films back to back. This experience would involve me, mum and Hermy, sometimes with my cousin and aunty lounging on the settee, getting the blankets out and eating Bombay mix or other Indian snacks. Looking back now, it was actually a really lovely time, glazed with lots of giggles and fun. A time of escape, from our own reality. Mum loved to watch the fashion and listen to the serious dialogues, which she would then recite to us, during moments of childish manipulation. For children, it encapsulated the wonderment of thinking 'Maybe this is how life is or could be.' Whenever there was a 'passionate scene', we were always told to close our eyes. My brother would always cover his eyes, with his fingers wide open!

This romanticised and unrealistic view of the world was formed over several years and I thought that maybe one day I'd be swept off my feet and meet the love of my life. I envisaged a Bollywood style struggle of some sort, but our love would save the day. Sadly, none of this happened, yet.

6th June 2016: Just feel extremely sad. The tears could not be contained – I was overflowing. Hurting. A pain that lingers. Although people don't intend to hurt, every comment cuts.

During my earlier years, I dated but have only experienced deep love once. No one had ever showered me with so many beautiful flowers, surprised me by driving hundreds of miles to wait outside my door, sing to me down the phone and write me poetry. He really made me feel like he would be the one I've been waiting for my entire life. He would be my husband. A man I used to think about when I was a teenager and wonder what he would be doing right now? Our relationship was far from perfect, but he gave me the experience of feeling loved and all that it comes with. Unfortunately, it never materialised the way I had hoped. We do both love and care about each other but it didn't work out. Life doesn't. It throws you off course. Redirects you, takes you through dark tunnels and detours all the way. We almost made it but not quite. I couldn't wait any longer. When the man you love and want to spend the rest of your life with tells you "You'll be on maternity leave by this date and we'll go on honeymoon here," you believe them, right? Why wouldn't you? Why would you say things like that, create hope, and then not follow up with action? I couldn't understand or make sense of words that had no meaning. As now infamously said, 'Words matter.' If someone spoke to me about a future, I would believe them and think that their intention is to have a future. Why else would you say that? I was wrong. I've since learned that to some people, words are just that. Empty. Meaningless. That's something I never really understood. It caused me a lot of pain and anguish. I had a long term relationship, which ultimately lead to nothing. No marriage, no divorce. No child. Nothing. All that aside, I did experience deep love. We do both care about each other. It just didn't last my lifetime. On reflection, and out of the 'love bubble', we assume people are the way *we* are – honest, loyal and holding the same values of a decent human being, but they are not. Like all relationships, I had some great and not so great times. Mum and my brother were never great fans of him, but always told me if I was happy, they were. Whilst I don't want to tarnish all men with the same brush, it has certainly closed off part of my heart, in fear of experiencing this kind of pain again and makes me question people's genuine intentions and sincerity, despite what they say. But I realise I have to open my heart again, in order to experience love again, even at the risk of getting hurt again.

I never shared my 'love-life' with many people – now I'm writing a book about it! It was interesting to observe though, because if you've not made your relationship 'public' and it's not been on display, be it on social media, or you've not held an event that the world knows about, people assume you haven't experienced love or anything associated with that life experience. I actually enjoyed the privacy of those years. It was our time. I had some magical moments with him. No one needs to know, apart from those that matter to me like mum and my brother and a couple of close friends. It's nice to know it was just about me and him. After it all ended and I reflected, it was hard for me to understand how one day you can love someone so much, you talk to them every day, several times a day, share everything with them, to then having no contact and becoming complete strangers. It was a difficult adjustment and transition to make. Having said that I've never been the type to stay friends with an ex. Once it's over, it's over and everything disappears.

Growing up in an Indian household, the pressure had always been there to get married and settle down. The minute you graduate and get a decent job, the silent alarms are heard out loud and in your head. Mum has been desperate for my marriage to take place. It's getting kinda tiring now. It's been a way she defines her own success – by me being married and settled. This is just a mindset that no matter how much I try to influence, cannot be changed. So, I guess I feel somewhat responsible for her yet unfulfilled desire. However, we are both clear, that I will not just 'marry someone for the sake of it', due to time pressure or fear of loneliness.

Over the years I remember always being the gooseberry. My friends would say 'Ramen can be the matchmaker,' 'Ramen can come along to meet the friends' boyfriends and hang around whilst they spend time together.' When everyone else was in a relationship, I always felt like the odd one out. Most of my friends and family my age are now married and have kids. I felt like I didn't belong. My own insecurities surfaced. However, the once ugly duckling then grew into a beautiful swan, who then grew to love herself more. She learned to nurture herself, be kind to herself and spend time with herself. During this process, I became me. I found Ramendeep. The wonderful me. I love spending time with myself. Not alone. I don't feel lonely. I feel secure in myself. I travel with myself, treat myself and do what feels right for me. I'm not someone who cannot be on my own. Far from it.

As I've had time to reflect on me and understand myself more, I understand that my craving and need for a man stemmed from the absence of my father's role in my life. He was there, but not actively present, in ways you'd expect from a father. I love my dad. He did what he knew. If he knew better, he'd do better. So, it's ok. I longed to be protected and looked after. Being the youngest in my family, I had to grow up very quickly and take on a lot of responsibilities. Not having a consistent male presence in my life has forced me to do things others would stereotypically, rely on men for – DIY, gardening, painting, buying cars, lifting heavy items without help, etc. With a curious mind, I always seek to learn, to try and figure it out myself. As a result, I don't have that reliance on a man do get things done and am confident to do things myself. My independence flourished.

Most importantly, for me I witnessed a terrible marriage and will try my best to avoid that at every cost. My brother always told me 'Don't be in an abusive relationship.' I will not allow that to happen.

Right now, given all that I have been through I am content with being with me. If someone comes into my life, great. If not, it's ok too. My life will still continue to blossom. I have officially surrendered.

24th Nov 2016 – The tears won't stop. They're flooding my soul. My heart is hurting so much. Feels like a daze. Not real. Like I'm floating and not really here. I want to feel like me again. I want to smile and be happy again. Right now, I can't eat, sleep. Just exhausted. I'm so tired.

Every time I was in tears, which was quite often, my mum would always want to console me. I didn't want her to and wanted to be left alone. She'd always say *'Your pain is mine. If you're sad, I'm sad. If you're happy, I'm happy'* She always saw her children as an extension of herself.

Society's expectations around marriage are so engraved in people's mindsets, that it really is a tough one to change. Don't get me wrong. It used to be what I wanted. It didn't work out for me yet, so I am forced into a position which is less than ideal. Having said that, just because you're not married or have children by a certain age or chose not to, doesn't mean you're any less of a person. We all know this theoretically, but we still judge. We still preach. I've been told by those who know me, 'You don't need a big car, you don't need a big house. It was interesting when I brought a house, people said is it 2 or 3 bedrooms? Assuming I didn't need anything bigger. I brought bigger. I work damn hard and I'll get it because I can and want it for me! 'You have all the time in the world, because you don't have children.' People, including those you know and don't, can be so cruel. It's so important to practice kindness and think before you speak. Try putting yourself in someone's situation before commenting.

Even my non-Asian friends would question why I wasn't married too. People would assume there's 'something wrong'. I'll set the record straight – there is nothing wrong. I am fully functional and a lovely person. Accept it. Don't try to understand or make sense of someone else's fate. No one else can 'fix' someone else's destiny. Besides, there are so many ways people can become families. Marriage and being a birth mother are not the only options.

I may have made some bad choices in life and mis-judged people. That does not mean I punish myself for the rest of my life. We all do what we know at the time. I had to forgive myself because I did what I knew at the time and believed in love and that it would work out. So many women do. I had to look at myself in the mirror and say 'It's ok.'

However, the world continues to judge. Sometimes it's worst from those that know you, but it just gives their idle minds something to talk about and discuss, because their own lives lack so much. Some assume it's because I'm so close to my mum. My mother is an independent lady, who is more than self-sufficient. I have learnt to slowly turn down and switch off the background noise. Then they take offence if you don't marry someone they suggest. So, they fabricate lies, to suit their agenda. I'm actually quite good at telling people to F off now, in a diplomatic way of course. But since my recent life event, I'm not even so diplomatic in my approach anymore.

I am strong enough to say no and I have a voice. A mind of my own. A stance. A decision that I can make about my life, in my time. I have rejected guys and guys have rejected me too and that's all ok. That's how it is. I know many couples who are together, but unhappy. Some people are scared to be alone. I don't have that issue and will only make a decision if it feels right for me and him. Mum panics and says 'Time's running out' or 'No one's perfect' etc. I understand all this but I will not give into pressure to live a life that pleases others. I do not have the disease to please. One time, I remember a relative saying 'The alarms are going off and you're not listening,' insinuating that my time to get married and have kids is almost over and I'm not doing anything. It was a very hurtful thing to say. Perhaps some people's intentions are good and they want to help or see me married, but they just go about it the wrong way. Ultimately it's god that has the final say, not man. Given all that I have been through, I'm searching for someone to really understand me. Like old souls reunited. I'd love that! One thing I do know for sure is that I will not marry someone just for the sake of it or because I am getting older. I have seen first-hand how the wrong partner can have a detrimental effect on not just you as a partner, but on generations to come. This will not be me. I have faith and believe in god's timing. I will not give up on love just because I haven't found it yet. I may have met shark-infested souls, but deep down in my pure soul, I know that good people, kind people do exist. I may have bruises on my heart and scars on my soul, but I can and always have the courage to continue.

We're always one decision away from changing the course of our lives. I remember being 24 and dating a guy who wanted me to move to the States – well, Malibu. Yes, I know! The first time we spoke on the phone, the conversation lasted for seven hours! I know I can talk, but that was something special. Anyway, I said no, because I did not want to move to another country. This single decision changed the trajectory of my life to this day. I sometimes think about what life would have been like had I said yes.

In Jan 2018, I started having counselling about my relationship and where I was in my life, aged 40 with no marriage or children. These days I know it's not such a big deal, but for me it was. I told her my full experience and how much I had invested in the man I loved so very much. She said it was an 'enormous loss'.

If I thought the breakdown of my relationship was bad, I could never have imagined what was in store for me in 2019…

2019, Infinity

'She wears hell so well, that no one can see the pain she's in.'

Reggie Nulan

Quote from my journal

31st Dec 2018
I got Hermy a wall calendar and was adding stickers to special
dates for him. He said put a sticker on the 10th Jan, that's
when I get some extra money…

Tuesday 1st Jan 2019
'Good morning! Today is the first day of a brand-new year. I'm
feeling good. It's going to be a great one. I know it. I declare it.
This year I'm already blessed with what's ahead. I can't wait to
find out – Let's do this!'

I couldn't have been more wrong. 2019 was a year I experienced a level of endless excruitiating pain, that I never knew existed.

3rd Jan, my beloved brother went to the barbers and didn't tell me. Went I noticed he wasn't in the house, I said in a panic, 'Where did you go Hermy?!! I couldn't find you and was looking for you everywhere.' Like a lost child. He laughed and said 'Aww Rummy I only went to get my haircut. I replied 'Don't leave me Hermy.' His reply was 'I'll never leave my Rummy.' Though grown up adults, we've always behaved like children. It's our way of expressing our love.

The same evening, H was sat up in bed. 'What's the matter?' I said in concern. 'Got pain in my chest Rummy.' 'Right, let's go the doctors.' 'No, I'll sleep it off, he said. Think I need to rest it off.' I then went to work and returned with some paracetamol and Lucozade. I poured it for him and helped him drink it, in my mothering style, even though I'm his younger sister. I've always been like that. Doing everything for him. Spoiling him as much as possible - making his room, his food, organizing holidays, packing his luggage etc. I enjoyed it. I wanted to protect him. Always.

Saturday: I've got some assessments for work and was revising, before planning to go to away for a whole week. Hermy came down the stairs and said, 'It's come back Rummy.' The pain in his chest. He then drove to the local walk-in centre and returned with some stronger painkillers. I asked what they said. His reply was 'They said it's muscular and I need to rest.' That seemed to work, for the time being. The nurse sent him home and all was fine. I now wish I'd gone with him to the walk-in centre. Herman is always polite and obliging, believing they are the 'experts'. I would've pushed for further investigations.

Sunday 6th Jan, I remember being really, really upset. Like sobbing on the floor, in my room. I didn't know why. My brother came into my room and asked what happened. I had no answer. Now it feels like a premonition for what was to come…

It was a Wednesday morning, 9th Jan 2019. All was well. I remember looking at the clock. It was 10am and I just left the house to go to work. In the car, I was chatting to a colleague about the Xmas' holidays and returning to work. Meanwhile, mum was trying to reach me on the phone. I couldn't take the call, as I was on the other line, so ignored her call. Normally, she calls for something non-urgent or a chat. She called again. I parked up, to text her saying 'text me'. She texted back saying 'the ambulance is here'. I called her straight back and she told me she'd called an ambulance and that my brother H, was on his way to hospital, as he was having difficulty breathing. I quickly turned back from where I was heading and called the hospital, from my car. I asked if he had arrived. The receptionist said, 'We have a 42 year old en route.' That was him. It took ages to find a parking space. Always does when you're in a hurry, or at least seems that way. I was going around and around until one became available. My heart was racing. The time was around 10:42am.

I went straight to A&E. I approached the desk and said I was the sister of Mr Dhoot. They said he's in resus. With my eyes filling up, I asked if he was in cardiac arrest. I got no reply but was told I could go through. I looked through the window of the door, which required access. I saw my beloved on a stretcher, awake but uncomfortable. The nurse was trying to hold him back, to get the ECG sensors on him. I saw her use a bit of force, which made my blood boil. I banged on the door and said, 'I've witnessed you be aggressive with my brother.' She explained that he is agitated and needed him to maintain his full weight on the bed. I waited there with him, whilst they carried out their tests. When I asked what they thought was going on. They weren't sure, so made assumptions about various things. They couldn't be sure until all his vitals would be stable. I told them about the chest pains earlier and asked them to do a CT scan. They didn't. Instead, they did a CT of the head, because he was confused and agitated. 'Unfortunately, we see this a lot,' one doctor explained. 'See what?' I asked, without paying attention to her response. The nurse then flashed a light into his eyes to show me his pupils were constricted. No one explained any further and I wasn't thinking straight anyway. I could tell how uncomfortable that was for him, but he couldn't say. I just went along with what they were saying, assuming they knew what they're talking about.

Mum was at home and couldn't rest. So I asked her to get a taxi, cos she was too anxious to drive. All the while, mum and I are texting each other. I stayed with H throughout the time he was in A&E. With tears in my eyes, watching him in pain, I said 'I love you.' I'd call him Eddie – our little secret. So, when the doctors couldn't get his full attention, I said 'Eddie' out loud. They said is his name Herman or Eddie? I smiled and said it's Herman.

He was conscious but I could sense he was struggling and in pain. He asked for water and I gave him a cup full, which he drank straight away. He seemed agitated and confused. The hospital beds were lining up in the corridors. In resus, there were two other patients either side of my brother. One was a young woman, who externally looked fine and was talking to someone on her mobile, but visibly upset. The other patient I think was an older man. He didn't seem serious either. So, I, assumed they didn't require immediate medical attention. All I know is that they were breathing on their own and didn't have several doctors surrounding them. At the time, my Hermy was the most serious. I then vaguely recall overhearing someone saying a bed was needed for someone coming in with sepsis. I know how dangerous sepsis can be, as my mum once had it and outcomes are time dependent. I now believe that her life was saved, when my brother was moved. It seemed to be a busy day. Junior doctors were looking after my brother. They eventually managed to settle him and told us he is now stable. What a relief! My heart had been on a knife-edge all that time. I didn't expect anything would be life-threatening but felt it would take several hours to be seen. So, I thought at least he's out of any immediate danger and once rested, we can go home.

We are told to go to cubicle 13, where Herman would be brought in. Sure enough, a few mins later, his bed was wheeled in and we were informed we'd be leaving once he's rested and well enough to leave. Mum and I were by his side. I was thinking when he's ready, we'll get a bite to eat on the way home because we were all so tired. Herman seemed restful and quiet. After about ten mins, he got up slightly and said 'Let's go home,' with a sort of strained and weak voice. Unknown to us, these would be his last words. I asked for a nurse to have a look and said 'Call a doctor.' Next thing we knew, he took three deep agonal breaths and his eyes rolled back. I screamed and said 'Call a fucking doctor!!' I said his name and felt sweat on his forehead. Mum looked at her son in disbelief – 'His lips have gone purple,' she said as desperation filled her voice. A mother watching her son fade in front of her own eyes, without any notice is an unbearable moment.

Then, all hell broke loose. A junior doctor walked past and came in to see what all the fuss was about. He searched for a pulse. It was rapidly fading. He banged the red button by Herman's bedside and sounded the emergency alarm. I have no idea where mum went. I was on the floor of the hospital corridor. I must've been screaming and shouting because all I remember was seeing a patient on a bed, covering her ears with her hands, at the scenes that were unfolding with my brother. Outside the cubicle there was absolute chaos and pandemonium. I was mad that things had got to this stage. The nurses were trying to get me off the floor. I think at some point, they had to drag me into a room – the family room.

I think mum was already in there. She was sat on a chair, with her arms and body wide, as if she'd just been cut open. They said, 'Sit with your mum.' They said they were doing all they could and would be back. I had faith. It will all be ok. We are in the right place, at the right time. All that could be done will be done. I had hope. I couldn't stand up but do vividly remember kneeling on the floor and praying. Praying really hard, whilst rocking back and forth in an attempt to regulate my dysregulated state. My faith was strong. I thought God isn't going to do this. He wouldn't do this to us. He can't be that cruel, as desperation flooded every cell in my body. We're only a small family – just the three of us. Our family should be growing not receding. We always described ourselves as 'one heart' – each of us making up the shape of a heart. We are sooo close. We love each other sooo much. God wouldn't do this to us. We've had our fair share of pain. I only have one brother. One sibling. Mum only has one son. Now it was time to enjoy life and make up for lost time and love. We're only a small family and love each other so deeply. God will save him. Everything will be ok.

Meanwhile, mum knew. Her maternal instinct kicked in. She knew. I kept saying, 'He's going to be ok mum'. It's all going to be ok. Mum didn't say anything but just kept shaking her head from side to side.

We waited. I'm unsure of how long they tried what they did. I looked at the nurse who had been with my brother from the start of his admission. I looked her in the eye and said, 'You said he's going to be ok? You said.' She looked at me with tears in her eyes. They were red and I knew she'd been crying before she came to see us.

I think about 40 mins later, the doctor came in and said, 'I'm sorry we couldn't save him.' He continued: 'We gave CPR, tubes etc. We tried everything.'

Umm… WHAT??? At this point, I felt like I had floated and started having an out of body experience. Like I was observing what was taking place. All I remember saying was NO. NO. NO!!! I didn't say anything else.

He'd been in hospital since 10:30am. By midday, he was stable and we were ready to go home. What the hell has happened?!! They came in and said 'We couldn't save him…'

What??? I distinctly remember the A&E doctor looked at me and said 'My brother died when he was 26.' Huh? Nothing is going in. I am in complete shock. I've zoned out of the room and this is now an out of body experience, where I feel like I'm watching some scary film. Still now, writing this, it feels like I'm writing about someone else. Doesn't seem real. Now I know my brain was protecting me. Whilst I was experiencing overwhelming trauma, my brain was blocking the memory and forming disassociation or detachment from reality.

I said 'Can we see him?' We went into a separate room. There he was lying on a hospital bed, covered in a white sheet. Only around 40 mins before we were with him, ready to go home. What am I doing here, in this room, with my beloved in this state?!!

Then it began. Mum started hitting herself. I have tears in my eyes writing this. I have never ever seen my mother in this way in my entire life. This is her first born. Her only son. Her everything. A part of her body, as she always described us. She made fists and just started hitting her thighs, which by the night were bruised black and blue. She continued, whilst screaming his name. The injustice of her son passing before his mother was palpable. She always affectionately called him

Honey. At one point, she screamed 'Honey' over him loud enough that his eyelids flickered and opened slightly. For a second mum thought he'd come back. The nurse then came and closed his eye.

I remember pulling at Herman begging him to wake up. Holding on so tight the nurses worried that I may tear his skin, which was still warm. Still soft, as it always was. All that was in that room at that time was a completely devastated and broken mother and sister, simply not wanting to let go of the only man in their lives. A nurse watched on, as she struggled to control her tears.

He was still wearing his rakhri, which I tied on him six months before. It's a decorated red bracelet, which, in India a symbol of love and protection between a brother and sister.

Unsure of date I wrote this, but entered in 9th Jan 2019:

2:17pm… Today my world fell apart…

Someone once said to me, when something so catastrophic happens, it will change the chemicals in your brain. It did. My brain and every fibre of my being has changed, since this date.

Family members arrived to take us home. I don't remember anything of the journey from the hospital, home. All I remember is I couldn't really get out of the car and someone was holding me. As I approached the house, I do remember falling on the wall outside my house and releasing the loudest gut-wrenching scream possible. The roar of pain rose from the pit of my soul. I screamed with my heart and roared with my soul. So much so, the neighbours came to see what had happened. Next, my legs turned to jelly and I could not stand. I was carried in. Once inside, the house I kept saying 'No, no, no, no.' That's the only words I could say. Whilst shaking my head and waving my arms out, I repeatedly shouted, 'NO, no no.' The paramedics were called. They wanted to sedate me, saying I was having a 'psychotic episode'. A paramedic loudly shouted towards me to say 'He's D!' I could have punched him. I now know they had to just say it how it was.

That first night was exactly like a nightmare. The brain fails to compute the real events taking place. We had family staying with us. In the middle of the night, I would wake up in a sweat, not able to make any sense of what was going on.

That first night I felt like I was having an out of body experience. I remember closing my eyes, falling asleep for a bit, then waking up, in the middle of the night and completely freaking out. It was the most surreal experience of my existence.

Mum said she'd had a dream about Hermy, where she physically felt him, on the night of the 9th Jan. In her dream she said, worried, 'Oh honey, where did you go?' He said, 'I'm right here mum. I haven't gone anywhere.' That was her first visitation dream. She also had another dream not long after of a new born baby. Perhaps he has taken new life. That's what she thought.

The next day, I somehow managed to drive to the hospital shaking and walking around there aimlessly, like a lunatic. I walked around the hospital shaking like a leaf, searching for answers. I didn't get any.

Once my beloved was released to us, my cousins supported me to go and see him in the mortuary. I remember banging on the door, as if to suggest why the hell is he in there?!! The lady brought him out on a metal trolley. Cold. Oh my god... no... my desperate tears and heart felt like it'd been cut open. NOoooo. I held him so close. With tears streaming down my face, I read the last pages he'd been reading from his bible. I'm unsure if he read everything on the pages of his bible, which was left open, but I recall some profound and relevant scripture: Psalm 69; *I pray to you lord, in the time of your favour; in your great love O god; answer me with your sure salvation. Answer me Lord, out of the goodness of your great love; in your great mercy turn to me.*

Psalm 70: *Hasten, O God, to save me; come quickly lord to help me.*

In those moments of reading the Psalms, I knew for sure god was very close and had in fact rescued my beloved.

Although, we are a Jatt Sikh family, Hermy got close to Christ, over the years. It was his way of connecting to god, understanding scripture and having hope by being saved. Family were fine with it and respected each to their own. I took a photo of the lord and his crucifix and tied it to his neck. I just sat there, sobbing, with his head in my arms, holding him tight. I'll never let go.

Over the coming days, the house flooded with relatives, friends and strangers. Mum kept saying 'He's been snatched from me. Just like that. Snatched by sudden death.' All shocked by what had happened. Amongst them was the man I'd loved with every inch of my being. He came in, first hugging mum, then me. I was doing everything myself and couldn't help but think had my husband been by my side, the weight of all this pain could have been carried and shared by him. As we separated from the crowd of people, he tried to comfort me, which was near impossible. He then said 'Snap out of it.' Although, I was numb, I felt that deeply. This man never had much emotional intelligence or empathy, which was all confirmed in this one heartless sentence. I knew in that moment I could never be with someone who fails to feel. I felt anger – how can you say something like that to me?! Can anyone even begin to comprehend what the hell has just happened?! No, you cannot!! It was clear this person wouldn't be there for me at my lowest, so didn't deserve me at any other time.

I remember someone else coming to the house saying 'You ok, Ramen? Smiling, saying 'You ok?!' I looked at her and said, 'No I'm NOT ok!!' Why are people like that?! What is going on?! I would never say things like that!! When people asked me how I was, all be it with good intentions, it made me angry, because I thought, well how do you think I am??!! My soul was in flames. Suddenly, being asked 'How are you?' felt like one of the most difficult questions to answer.

Three days later, on Saturday, my mum wanted to take a long bath. Something compelled me to stay with her, in the bathroom. I stayed with her, whilst she finished. Next thing I know, she slowly, silently closed her eyes and started to fade into the water, slowly reducing her breathing. It was like she wanted to be at peace, with her son. I screamed 'Mum!' My cousin and aunts rushed in to save her. I meanwhile, ran outside the house and ran out onto the street, having thought my whole world had disappeared, just like that. In that moment, I felt like my world was on fire. My mum went into a diabetic coma, in the bath. That was it. My tiny but entire world was now ablaze. I did not want to live. It was that extreme. I couldn't begin to process the unfolding events.

I went to see mum, in hospital and it was all déjà vu. I hated every part of it. I actually went to Cubicle 13 in A&E and said to the receptionist, 'This is where it happened.' As if I wanted to lay blame somewhere and someone. I was seeking revenge. That hospital seemed the right place, even though I got no answers. No one will accept responsibility.

After a few days in hospital, mum was back home, recovering. My friend Neelam really came forward to help, when I felt most helpless.

I, on the other hand started suffering from extreme hyperventilation, shortness of breath, panic attacks and tremors. This was coupled with sleepless nights, for months on end. The impact on mum was screaming in her sleep, in the middle of the night. Every time I'd try to sleep, I'd be woken from my slumber by mum's aching screams. They still echo in my ears now.

I remember we couldn't get a date for my beloved's service, because the coroner's office was so busy. The post-mortem took a couple of weeks. I thought about all those families in pain. There was no covid at this time.

Now it was down to me to arrange everything. To give my beloved brother the best, most fitting tribute that he deserves.

I don't remember getting dressed properly or combing my hair to drive or go into town. Don't remember eating or drinking. Felt like my body was starved of the love from my one and only sibling. I went into autopilot. I had to do EVERYTHING the way that HE would have wanted and I wanted to make his journey to the lord amazing. I got some comfort from the fact that he loves the lord and that he was at peace.

Not sure how I made it into town, but I remember Valentine's Day was approaching, so there were lots 'love' products on sale. I brought a cream teddy bear, holding a heart, with 'I love you.' We were all very expressive about our love. Nothing would change that now. I brought one for him and one for myself. I also brought red and gold heart confetti to go with him. Anything I could find, to make the whole thing as special as possible. Walking like a zombie in town, trying to make sure I didn't miss anything, so I just brought plenty of everything.

One of the hardest parts was buying his clothes for his final journey. I remember doing the same for my dad. I chose a dark blue suit, blue shirt and tie. Black shoes and turquoise socks. I brought cards with rainbows on them and Valentine's Day cards from me and mum. We celebrated Valentine's Day, because it's all about love and we love love. It was strange writing the cards to him, but I'm glad we did. I can't believe how I did all that, on my own. I don't know how I got through each day and put one foot in front of the other. God's grace was surrounding me for sure. There were lots of family around, but I felt like I knew him best and I wanted to do it his way.

Around one week after the event, I remember receiving a call from the coroner's office. I was alone in the car. I parked up on a side road. She said 'Are you ready to hear the outcome of the report?' I took a deep breath and said yes. She told me it was a 'ruptured aortic aneurysm'. Wow. I didn't know what I thought she'd say, but certainly not that. I was angry. I had asked them to do a chest Xray or a CT-scan of his chest. They didn't. Months later, a hospital investigation stated 'You don't expect a 42-year-old healthy male to have this, so they didn't look for it.' To me, it's unbelievable that they didn't even consider it an option. It was later found that an opportunity had been missed.

January 20^{*th*}

I went to see my beloved today. He enjoys Sundays. A day of peace and prayer. I held his hand and rubbed it, to make it warm. I managed to do it for a short time. I prayed. Read several prayers, for those close to the lord. Then played 'Jesus Loves You' and 'Never Forget You'. During my hour, again I told him how much I love him. I held him tight and prayed. All this was with endless tears.

For the service, mum wasn't in any state to do anything, so I planned it all. All I remember thinking was, it has to be the best. It would be a white horse drawn carriage, with white feathers. A white box (still struggling to say/write some of the language related to the situation). There would be floral tributes in the form of a heart made of deep red roses, a gateway to heaven, a crucifix, a khanda (Sikh religious symbol), 'son', 'brother' and nephew. I wanted a condolence book, candles, star confetti and a memory tree.

I made several calls to arrange a videographer and trawled through hundreds upon hundreds of photos, to find the ones that represented our love the most. There were so many to choose from. I chose his songs, and prepared my speech. The chosen songs were 'Chithi Na Koi Sandesh' (No letters or any news); 'I'll Be There' (Mariah Carey) and 'I Am Free' (Mariah Carey).

I don't think I slept for around three days straight, as the day of my beloved's service was approaching. It had to be perfect for him, as he made his journey to the Lord. Getting ready for the final journey. I didn't sleep at all. Finished my speech at around 4am.

25th Jan 2019

6am – The room had all been cleared out of furniture. Family and friends had started to arrive. It was a cold dark January morning, but the sun was starting to rise. I waited outside for my beloved. I could hear the horses' hooves clicking, before I could see them. The sight of beautiful white horses was all I could see, as they trotted around the corner of my street. I couldn't place my brother into what was in the carriage behind them. The two somehow wouldn't connect in my mind. Lots of family had already gathered inside and outside the house. The men reached out to bring H home. I wanted to carry him too. I tried, although I was crushed between tall, strong men. One thing I know for sure though is that he loved being in that horse and carriage. I know that. He was carried into our home, which would be his last physical presence – in our childhood home, where we survived so many highs and lows. I don't remember much, apart from placing one of the two teddy bears with him and keeping the other for myself. I sprinkled stars and heart confetti inside with him. At the same time, sobbing uncontrollably. Mum kept gracing his face. I was going through the motions, but I was aware that I had to make it the best it could be, for him. Nothing else would be enough.

We arrived at the chapel, as the carriage is pulled up. I later saw a photo taken of me, holding a single yellow rose and carrying a deep aching expression on my face. I don't remember the actual moment but can connect with the pain of that day.

We walked in on the entrance music 'Woh lamhe'/'Those times'. I couldn't believe it… his face and name were on the screen. My H. Oh my. What am I witnessing? Everything was fine a few days ago!! This simply cannot be real. It all felt like I was observing, whilst going through an out of body experience again. Going through the motions without being present.

Everyone made their way in. The west chapel was packed with over 200 people. The ardās, an Indian prayer, took place, followed by a song mum chose. The screen then changed to a series of photos with mum and H. I heard her groan whilst clutching her stomach and folding forwards. The aching despair of a mother witnessing the worst of life's harsh realities.

Then it was my turn to take the stage. My family were telling me I wouldn't be able to write a speech, let alone read it in front of hundreds of people. I had no doubt. He was always my focus and I would never let him down. I will do it and I did do it. I just don't know how. It felt as though God had lifted me through the pit of pain to enable me to read my speech with confidence and without error.

Speech:

Friday 25th Jan 2019 – A Service of Love & Gratitude for Herman Dhoot

Family, friends, and loved ones. Those who have travelled from near and far – Thank you for gathering with us today, in our moment of indescribable, unimaginable pain. A loss of such magnitude, it's unbearable to even comprehend. The thought of a future without the physical presence of my beloved brother Herman is inconceivable. My brother. My heart. My best friend. My world. My Hermy. My Eddie.

Born in the same month, we were more like sensory twins, that just siblings. I'd know what he was thinking and feeling and vice versa. We had one heart. One heartbeat. No words needed.

When my brother was born, it was our Harpal bhuaji (aunty) that named him Har-man, which means every heart – I know for sure he's got a place in everyone's heart. Everyone that knew Herman had a fond memory of him. I called him 'My Hermy', or more recently 'Eddie' – a name that only he and I knew the meaning behind. That will remain between us. Mum would tell me stories of how good looking he was as a baby and how people would stop her in town and say what a beautiful boy he was, big brown eyes and a cheeky smile, which he still has today. Yes, he always got more attention than me.

At school, I was always known as 'Herman's sister', never really owning my own identity but always living in his shadow. This is something I was acutely aware of and secretly proud of, but rarely showed. Why wouldn't I be proud to have a big brother, who's extremely popular, good looking and intelligent, so of course I'm going to be the protective yet proud little sister.

*To describe my beloved Herman as intelligent would be an understatement and an injustice to his mind. Herman was **exceptionally gifted**. He had an IQ of a **genius**. He was invited to join MENSA. – an elite society specifically for the UK's intellectuals, boasting some of the smartest brains on the planet. I spoke to Mensa only yesterday, after making some enquires. The lady confirmed the Herman had taken the IQ test on the 30th*

April 1994, aged 17. She confirmed he indeed qualified in the top 2% of the UK's intellectuals. I'll repeat that – my beloved brother Herman had an IQ of 153 (off the scale for 98% of the population) He qualified with a score, in which only the top 2% of the UK population achieved – that's a population of over 60 million people. Not many people can say that. The average IQ is between 100 and 140. To put his score into perspective, he was only a few points short off Albert Einstein and Stephen Hawkins. I'm so proud of him.

I never saw Herman revise for any exam, almost ever. He would get straight As without even having to touch a textbook. Only a few months ago I printed out his GCSE certificates and framed them for him. This was to remind him of his unique brain. We recently joked about how he was in the top classes for everything and didn't have to work, meanwhile I had to beg him to help me with my homework. We both giggled.

*Herman's potential was huge. I remember teachers fussing over him, encouraging this raw uncarved talent to unleash. However, sometime during adolescent, he lost his way in life. His mental health declined and he slowly withdrew from the world. Like a butterfly on the cusp of greatness and ready to fly, he didn't quite make it. This was the fall from grace that he never truly recovered from. He lost interest in life and turned to God. His faith kept him going. Herman had his fair share of battles, **but I stood by his side through it all. I never gave up. Not once.** I couldn't. He's my Hermy. My everything. During those difficult years, it was a very testing time for our family. There wasn't anything I wouldn't do for him. I sought help from every possible avenue. I became and always will be Herman's champion. His advocate, his voice, his protector forever. I always did my best to attend all his appointments, meetings, manage his care plans, treatments and support. I'm sure I annoyed many professionals along the way, by demanding answers. He was always my priority. I made things happen to help him. There were times he made my life difficult too, but in my heart I knew that wasn't him. He needed help. **I didn't fight anger with anger, I fought it with love.** An abundance of love, so he never felt any lack.*

PAUSE.

Death shows up to remind us to live more fully, that's exactly what we did, when our dad went to sleep, and didn't wake up 14 years ago. Herman found dad dead, which naturally had a profound impact on him. The three of us became tighter than ever. It was sometimes during these conversations that I would say 'Eddie please look after yourself. I need you, don't leave me.' His response would be a tight cuddle followed by 'Aww... Rummy. I'm not going to leave you. Together forever.' He was very childlike. We talked about getting old together and what that would be like. We'd celebrate Valentine's Day together, because love is love. We knew the true measure of life is love. A life well loved, is a life well lived. A love and that is what is carrying us and breaking us at the same time. An absolute unwavering devotion to each other.

All he had to say was where in the world he wanted to go and I would make sure it happened. Hermy and I walked the streets of Japan, Hong Kong, Malaysia, Mumbai, Mexico, Thailand, New York, Dubai and Europe.

Herman was also a thrill seeker by nature. He loved Alton Towers, water parks and didn't hesitate to take a ride on the 'The Leap of Faith' – a 60ft vertical slide drop in Dubai.

One particular highlight was last Easter, when we went to Israel, a place close to Herman's heart. We visited Jerusalem and Bethlehem. We visited the room of the Last Supper, he touched the Star of David and the tomb of Jesus.

During what I now know to be our last holiday together in November, we were in Mexico. Looking back, it was such a magical memory. Me and my Hermy, up in a parachute gliding over the most beautiful blue and green sea, smiling, swinging our legs in harmony singing 'Come fly with me, let's fly lets fly away.'

Now he's gained his angel wings and flown to another world, but is still very much with me.

Life is not measured by how many breaths we take, but the moments that take our breath away. We had hundreds of those. The true measure of life is love. A life well loved, is a life well lived. Love is our legacy – timeless, boundless, endless love. It goes on forever.

When Hermy went to be with the lord, I felt like the unluckiest girl in the world, to lose my one and only brother. It was a brutal blow to my heart. However, I soon realised I wasn't unlucky at all. Some people don't have the love of any siblings. Then there are those who have many, but are not so close. For me, I was blessed to experience the abundance of pure, unconditional love with my Beloved Herman. We are a small family, but bursting with big hearts, full of love. I feel privileged that I dedicated and devoted years of service to my brother, without wanting anything in return. I did it because I wanted to. Because I care. I love him. I wanted him to experience a better quality of life. To give his life meaning and create magical memories forever. That is what I treasure most now.

Even though Hermy's life was improving, we shared so much love and he was starting to enjoy life again, I know deep down his soul was still restless. He wanted peace and prayed for that. When he went to be with the god, I felt immense anger that my brother was stolen from me. I prayed on my knees, in A&E, for him to be saved, but no one listened. I discussed this with my earthly sister Holly, and said Holly my faith let me down. Her response was, that's because his faith was stronger. That was a profound moment and one that's very true.

In the end he too knows how much I love him – that's why he kept his rakhri on (a bracelet that a sister ties on her brother for love and blessings, in the Indian culture). He never took the last one off. Even 6 months later he was still wearing it – he kept it on until his last breadth and beyond. He also kept old rakhris from previous years. Our love is tied forever and ever. Together forever Eddie. I love you so much. Always in my heart.

The greatest honour of my life is to be Herman Dhoot's sister. I will continue to make you proud.

My Hermy didn't like the word 'Goodbye', but instead preferred 'See you soon'…and this is how it will always be.

I cannot believe I am standing here, in our moment of deep despair, under these unimaginable circumstances, facing a mountain of pain ahead. Nothing will ever be the same again.

Thank you Hermy for all the love, cuddles, chaos, giggles and magical memories. This physical separation is unbearable and I will miss you beyond measure. I know you would never have left mum and I, in this devastating state. If you knew, you wouldn't have left us. At the same time, I take solace in knowing you are finally at peace, with the Lord.

The painful irony of all this is that it ended where you began. Life had come full circle. All was well until you were cruelly taken from us, that's how I feel. As for you, I can see you now smiling saying 'I made it Rummy.' I made it to heaven.

Thank you. God bless you.

Together forever Eddie. I love you forever and more.

Your 'Rummy' forever

My beloved was there, with the grace of God, making sure I didn't stumble. My earth sister, Holly stood by my side, in case I fell – I didn't.

After my song, our song, mine and my brother's song was played. It was I'll be there, by Mariah Carey. I would often sing this to him, reassuring him that I will always be there for him. Always.

This was then followed by Psalm 23, read by a priest, which Hermy loves:

The Lord is my shepherd, I lack nothing.
He makes me lie down in green pastures,
he leads me beside quiet waters,
he refreshes my soul.
He guides me along the right paths
for his name's sake.
Even though I walk
through the darkest valley,[a]
I will fear no evil,
for you are with me;
your rod and your staff,
they comfort me.

You prepare a table before me
 in the presence of my enemies.
You anoint my head with oil;
my cup overflows.
Surely your goodness and love will follow me
all the days of my life,
and I will dwell in the house of the Lord
forever.

Then, as he went on his final journey, I had the song 'I Am Free' played. This was followed by the release of three heart balloons representing us, three beautiful white doves and 42 blue balloons for his physical presence on earth.

It was a day, that I know he would have been overwhelmed by. The songs, the prayers, the horse and carriage. Only the best for my bestie. My Eddie. My love overflowed. It was a story of endless love. Love that overcame mental health, dysfunction, aggression and arguments. We walked the bridge of love that my mum built in our lives and I'm so glad we did. So many don't get the chance to make peace or show love. We made sure our love for each other was always on display – for us. No one else.

25h Jan 2019: 16 days…
Today went as well as it could. It's never final or farewell, but see you soon.

Over the coming days and weeks hundreds of people arrived at the house. All I heard was 'I'm so sorry for your loss.' Everyone said it. They all said the same thing. It was as though they were empty words that had no meaning. Hollow in their state. It made me realise how conditioned we are, as a society to behave and talk the same way. To follow the masses. To 'fit in'. It didn't feel personalised or thought through. When people said that to me, it made me angry because I thought I haven't 'lost' anything. No one can take my beloved brother away from me. Ever. He is and always will be my brother and a part of my life. Just because his body has physically stopped functioning and there is no longer a biological process taking place, by no means is he 'lost' or that my relationship with him ended. Nothing could be further from that. My beloved brother's presence is inextricably intangible. It cannot be described adequately. It can only be felt. I feel Hermy to this day. You will feel their presence and if you notice, you will get signs. The way I interpreted the situation is that he changed form. This adjustment is not an easy one to make and takes time. I believe we are energy, spiritual beings. He believed that too. That can never be destroyed. I felt compelled to change the 'lost' narrative. It's a term I no longer use and I never say 'I'm sorry for your loss' to those that grieve, unless they feel differently. To me it felt meaningless. I felt like people just follow the masses and it is the 'thing to say' as opposed to the appropriate word or sentence for that moment. This my personal experience and I don't impose it on anyone. My relationship with my brother continues and is eternal. Infinite in its state. I have a brother and he is very present in my life. I feel his energy. I talk to him and about him all the time. He is and always will be a part of my life. His name will always be mentioned and now the world too will know him. Energy does not die. I'm not in denial. I have accepted he is not physically here, but I and my beloved brother have always believed we are so much more. Our bodies are just our vessel. I actually asked him, when we talked about it before, how I would connect with him after his physical passing, he told me to look at the stars – that is what I do. It's amazing that every night I look into the night sky, there is now always one star which shines brighter than any other. The single bright star shows up in my bedroom window. I know he's around.

The actual truth is that I am the one who is lost. The compass of my life has gone. I couldn't connect with anyone who hadn't experienced what I had. I was angry with the world. Angry when people spoke to me about parent and grandparents, or someone who had a long illness. 'You don't fucking get it, I thought.' I stand by what I say, that one will never begin to understand unless they have experienced and witnessed a sudden bereavement, of a young person, the closest person to you in your life and endured the trauma of it all afterwards you will never be able to imagine, let alone understand the pain. My experience of my dad passing was very different. The fact that I wasn't there meant I don't relive the horrific scenes daily, as I do here. Terrible flashbacks haunt me.

26th September
Went back to the cemetery. The floral tributes still there. His name above them. Oh my! I stood in front of them, tears pouring down my face whilst the torrential rain drenched his coat I was wearing, whilst diluting and drowning my tears.

About a week after the service, I went alone to 'collect' him and bring him home. I was handed a large burgundy plastic jar, full of grey ash and white speckles. O-M-G. This is what is left of my almost 6ft, 42-year-old beautiful beloved brother. Naturally, I cradled the remanence of his physical matter, and came to my knees on the floor, as the tears and pain filled me once again. The enormity of the pain is like a tsunami erupting inside you. The woman in the room next door was peering out the window, having heard my anguish. I brought him home, and mum and I hugged what remained, so tight. Although, I know this is not truly him, but his vessel. But in that moment I thought that is what it all comes to when this life ends. All the things we buy, the experiences we have all boil down to this – that we return to dust. Our bodies are the single greatest possession we will ever own. Since then, I no longer feel attached to any material things. What once gave me joy, now does nothing for me. Buying 'things' does not make me happy. It's the experiences I have and the impact I can have on someone else's life is what matters, because now I always have the end in sight. That is ultimately everyone's legacy. So, I hope writing this book will touch lives and connect with you. After all, we all have the same feelings and heart inside.

The preparations then began to go to India. A place called Kiratpur is where we go to scatter the ashes of our loved one in line with tradition. Again, every detail was critical. I was meticulous in my search for the best products I could find for him. A heart-shaped gold urn, a star-shaped silver urn, an angel urn and the biodegradable rainbow urn. Everything had meaning. I prepared him with every bit of love and care. He loves glitter, which always made him smile, so I sprinkled lots of glitter and flowers with him, to make sure he still sparkled as his journey continued in flowing waters. That was one of the toughest journeys of my life. I was there but wasn't in the moment.

From early on, I was dreading the day when people stopped coming over, when everyone retreated back into their own worlds and the door would be closed to just me and mum at home. It kind of scared me. Those who know grief, know that the process doesn't actually begin until weeks, months and years after the event. And it stays. It changes shape and size, but that void is always there.

Mum was forcing me to go back to work after a few months off. Then it was suggested I needed counselling. I went to my first session with Cruse Bereavement. I remember arriving in my brother's coat, drenched in the rain, with my hood on, looking down. I didn't care what I looked like. I just remember sitting in front of the counsellor sobbing uncontrollably for 50 mins straight. When I caught a glimpse through my flooded eyes, I could see the anguish on the guy's face – just watching me in agony but not being able to do anything to ease my pain. I remember a friend saying they wish they could take my pain away or do something to ease it. At the time I couldn't think straight, but now I would say, just be there. You don't have to 'fix' the person, because you never will. Just let them know you are there and regularly ask them how they are coping – months and years after, not just over the first few days and weeks. Even as I write this, 33 months on, one thing I know for sure, absolute unquestionable surety is that grief never ends. The intensity of the pain may reduce but it's always there. You may not always say it, share it or think about it as often as you once did, but you will continue to feel it. An invisible scar that only you know and carry.

Over the coming months, profound grief consumed me. Like a new blood, seeping and flooding my body, whilst piercing every cellular and atomical level of my being, I felt like I had morphed into a fireball, raging with anger, burning through the injustice that had so abruptly torn through my small but desperately loving family. I remember being so mad, I said to my counsellor, I wish I could get a match and set the world on fire, such was my rage at the injustice of my life and the obliteration of my family.

The silence in the house was deafening. The emptiness so full. The void so huge. Grief leaked into everything I did in life, which meant I didn't want to do anything. Didn't want to go out, because I'd see him everywhere I'd go, I struggled to go out for meals, because he loved to do that. He loved holidays. However, going without his physical presence was torturing us every step of the way. Our first holiday since that day was just spent unable to control our emotions. Both, me and mum, holding onto each other to save one another from drowning in the ocean of pain that surrounded us.

Everything was always for three. Now that empty seat, plate, glass was left for two. This cut deep. For a while, and sometimes even now I do still order a table for three. Two just doesn't feel right.

Simple things like going to the supermarket, seeing things he eats, I still buy and eat them. There's a pain in going shopping, seeing men's clothes and wanting to buy them for him. I wear his T-shirts and hoodies all the time. People say I should give some of his clothes away. This is something I cannot do. I want to hold onto everything. I remember telling him off for having smelly feet. Now I've kept his trainers in a sealed bag, so I can smell his feet again.

One of the things I felt overwhelmingly was an immense feeling of grief for the life that could have been. Herman's life.

A genius. Invited to join Mensa with an IQ amongst the top 2% of the population. An incredible raw talent that could have changed the world. A musical genius, with limitless talent. I can't help but think he could have made a real name for himself on a global scale, be it in any area of science/astrophysics, medicine or music. It could have been music, which he had an incredible talent for. I can't help but draw comparisons with Albert Einstein – similar intelligence and passed away the same way. Albert Einstein quoted *'If I were not a physicist, I would probably be a musician. I often think in music. I live my daydreams in music. I see my life in terms of music… I get most joy in life out of music..'* That too is very much like my beloved.

This situation brought forth grief not just for the physical loss of a person I love so so much, but a life he could have lived. Grief for nieces and nephews ill never have. Only a couple of weeks before he said he'd like to have children. I know I would have soaked them in love. Grief for not having his physical presence in all that I do with my life moving forward. So, whilst you read this not knowing my beloved Herman, you know that he graced this earth with talent in abundance. **His name is Herman Dhoot. His legacy lives on, through me and now through this book.**

It made me think about all the people who are not able to fulfil their raw talent and gifts due to mental illness, trauma or a premature passing. All those who are here but not able to fulfil their amazing potential for whatever reason. Incredible lives that have been cut short and a talent unfulfilled. I think of you. They should never be forgotten.

There is also grief for me. A changed Ramen, who lost all joy in her life. I'd forgotten what it was like to smile, let alone laugh out loud. I'd lost me. I have fundamentally changed as a person and this event changed the trajectory of my life. So much of me evaporated, on Wednesday 9th Jan 2019.

Sometimes I feel like I've lived so many different lives in one life time. Played so many characters in so many different scenes. This is one of those life changing moments.

My rage was also fuelled by an injustice when I called several solicitors and explained what had happened to my brother, because I so desperately wanted answers and to apportion blame in some way. At the hospital, no one knew what was going on until it was all too late. They didn't know, because they failed to see. Failed to take notice of every opportunity. An opportunity that was missed. Surely, there was a case to be had for that negligence? However, every solicitor's firm I called said they wouldn't accept the case because basically it wouldn't generate any or enough money. That's basically what it boiled down to. I wanted to fight for his justice. Fight against those that I believe let him down, but I just didn't have it in me. My grief alone was debilitating enough. What can a young woman, experiencing overwhelming grief, on her own do? Maybe people make these kinds of matters so overwhelming and complex, knowing the griever won't have it in them to fight on. I couldn't take them all on. I didn't have the time, energy or mental strength to. The outcome wouldn't have changed, they all said. So, I let it be. Hermy would've have said the same – 'Leave it.' So, I did.

Over the coming months, my despair, fear and loneliness grew in abundance. I hit rock bottom. Felt a pain I didn't know existed, despite my dad passing 14 years earlier. This was something else. This is something I'd never experienced before. My heart had been ripped out and crushed. My heart experienced intense physical pain. Now its every beat has a new aching rhythm. It also burns flames of unfairness. I felt like I had been chopped in half. A forever state of anguish. A constant reminder of what's missing in life. Only a few weeks earlier, my beloved brother and I were talking about a future and getting old together, sitting in a care home reminiscing the 'good old days.' All that gone, just like that.

7th March
Just… unbelieveable…

8th March 2019
Mummy was really, really really sad today. Hermy, mum's screams and tears for you will haunt me forever. Never seen

*her in that state before. She went upstairs to your room
and lay with you in your bed – she was cradling her baby,
who was now in an urn screaming and crying. It was really
distressing to watch*

I became so obsessed with my brother that I kept wearing
his T-shirts and hoodies (still do some days), which brought me
great comfort. I didn't want to get up, go out. I isolated myself,
because no one understood. People just pissed me off with their
own stories, in a futile attempt to try and connect with me.
I was angry. Mad at the injustice of it all. This was a sudden
event. I saw it unfold in front of my eyes. It happened to the
most important man in my life. It's not the same as someone
who has a chronic illness or someone who was elderly. I am not
minimising anyone's pain. I know everyone experiences grief
differently and each pain is their own. But, for me, this was
different. This was deep, traumatic in it's nature and has left
an imprint of horrific memories and flashbacks that scar me
daily. From the minute I wake up to the moment I go to sleep,
the scenes are there. I try to escape them but they're there – on
replay. This was now going to be a part of my life. Like an
invisible life backdrop.

*6th April
H, I don't know what to say. I am totally and utterly stunned.
Just unbelievable. Don't wanna say 'Miss you,' cos that will
mean something is real, when I don't want it to be. I hope I don't
live in this suffering too long H – together forever remember. I
hate everyone and everything. Wanna hide. Sleep forever…*

H and I had already planned our holidays for 2019. One of
them was to Moscow. He wanted to see the Orthodox churches.
I didn't let the physical separation stop me. The holiday was
booked. I took H with me, in his golden star urn, always by
my side. The orthodox churches there were amazing, not to
mention Red Square, St Basil's Cathedral. I walked around Red

Square listening to Michael Jackson's 'Stranger in Moscow'. The lyrics so poignant. My brother's presence was strong and real. There was an empty seat next to me going there and one on the way back. His presence in that empty space couldn't have been more obvious.

17th April 2019
H, I know you were with me, because the seat next to me was empty. It's for you. You are here, there and everywhere – with me. I love you more than you can imagine. The moon was full of light. I see you.

18th April
I know you wanted to see the churches in Moscow. They are sooo beautiful. A lady, who saw me visibly upset said you haven't gone anywhere, but are very much here, with me. You are. The feeling is overwhelming, yet indescribable.

April 22nd Easter Monday
Jesus rose again. He said to Martha, 'Your brother will rise again.' Later, we travelled to India. Hermy, we travelled with you in full sparkle and colour. You sat in the middle, watching Bollywood film, Khuda Gawah.

24th April
Travelled to Kiratpur with my family in India.

Again, it very much felt like I was observing a situation I wasn't in. I went into autopilot and went through the motions. The eight hour plane travel to India was a very surreal and an anxious time. Just me mum and H. People trying to make small talk and us having to say what the purpose of our trip was without being able to muster up the words to say it, was not an easy task. I had to make sure everything went to plan and I kept him really, really close. Cuddled him tight, just like we always did, until it was time for him to be released and 'free.' The waters at Kiratpur are much clearer and cleaner than what they used to be, when we took dad there. I unveiled him from the luxury velvet cover, took the lid off his urn and began to sprinkle him. It was agonising but beautiful, as he was the only one that looked different. The only one that outshone the rest of the ashes, just as he did in life. He sparkled so bright amongst the glitter, as the sun shone on him and even more so as he drifted along the flowing waters, with flowers embracing him on the journey. I had to do everything with some exaggeration, to reflect his uniqueness. There was no way he would just blend in with everyone else. He stood out then, as he always did. He stood out now.

I had kept some of him with me at home. My request is that when I pass, he'll be mixed in with me too.

29ᵗʰ April
12am – Left to visit The Golden Temple, in Amritsar. My heart wasn't ready. I was angry with god, but we went as I didn't want to let mum down. There's no time of day that place is not busy. I found a place and sat alone. It was actually where Hermy and I stood together, the last time we went. I just stared into the water in front of me, trying to fathom what was happening, as tears filled my eyes.

Next thing I know, mum slipped on the floor and we thought she'd mildly hurt herself. Turned out, she'd suffered a full shoulder fracture and needed an operation. I know it was all a symptom of all the pain that's erupting inside her.

I remember we went to Bangla Sahib Gurudwara, in Delhi. We gathered fresh flowers and asked for a prayer to be done in my brother's name. We then walked into the main hall and neither mum nor I could control our emotions. Like a balloon ready to burst. This drew attention and people started asking what had happened. We told them, without telling them in full sentences. They understood. We were overflowing with tears all the way.

Whenever we'd be out, Herman would always hold mum's hand, as she'd recently had some back problems. It made her feel so secure. Her tall son, holding her hand tightly, with love and comfort. Now I felt obliged to do the same. To take some of that on myself, even though it would be different. I just couldn't hold it the way he did. He's tall, I'm not. He's got big hands, I haven't. Ultimately, I can't make up for him, no matter how much I tried.

2nd/3rd May
I've been seeing white butterflies Hermy… a sign

10th May, Delhi
Always book a table for three. That's how it was and always will be.

Back home, it was so strange. It was at this point, I think it all really began. I started looking into the details of what happened and how.

Below is an email I wrote to the healthcare professionals, supposedly 'looking after' my beloved:

29th May 2019
Hi

> *It's 03.22am. I cannot sleep.*
>
> *I'm struggling to carry on. I'm not depressed. I do not need pills. I am someone who is desperately sad. Like a raw nerve that's been severed. I'm hurting so so much. Herman is my world, yet you treated him in the most undignified manner. Making assumptions throughout. He is a genius that had a fall from grace. His IQ is in the top 2% of the population. He will never be referred to in the past tense.*
>
> *I will never recover from this. The flashbacks and trauma are never-ending. My screams at the hospital and at home disturb me daily. No counselling is working. What I witnessed, with the closest person to me in the entire universe was horrific. I am not sick. This did not need to happen. This should not have happened.*

I have a very poor quality of life now. I'm the one that lost my life that day. I have lost faith in everyone and everything. We will meet in due course.

20 weeks. 140 days. 4 months 20 days.

*3rd **June 2019** – Sobbing on your bed…*

*10th **June**: Early morning, woke up with tummy pains. Sat on the floor. Took pills. Hurts. Thought of you and the way you'd comfort me. Looked at my phone, it read 04:04am. I know it's an angel number, so I looked up what it meant. 'Angel number 04:04 means there are loving angels around you, so they will help you. It is very powerful.' My pain went immediately. H, thank you I love you sooooo much.*

*21st **June 2019** – Hermy, our aunty…♡*

Our beloved aunty passed away. She was such a huge part of our lives and loved Hermy so very, very much.

*12th **July** – Been seeing soo many angel numbers everywhere. Such a sign from the universe and God.*

*15th **July** – Throughout the day all I saw were angel numbers 08:08, 09:09, 11:11, 14:14, 15:15. I know you're right here with me.*

Later, I went for a drive, listening to a Hindi song, 'Tera Chehra'/('Your Face'). Next thing I notice from the clear blue sky, a feather falls, right in front of my eyes. Wow. It's incredible. Tears. I know it's you. I know.

*22nd **July***
All day's been hard. I decide to nap around 3:45pm. I had the deepest, most real visitation dream. You visited me Hermy in my deep state of sleep. You were in your thin blue hoodie, in

the kitchen. I was in the stairs. I stood there. Then you turned around, with a big smile on your face. You walked towards me and scooped me up in your arms, for a tight cuddle. I was in shock to see you. I held you so close. So tight. I felt immense relief. I said thank you – I'm glad that's over… sigh.

Then I woke up and panicked. In disbelief. Oh no….it was a dream

I looked up what had just happened. It says 'These are visitation dreams – telling you you're right here, close by.'

Over the past few months, I desperately connected with people who could understand how I was feeling – specifically those affected by sudden grief of a sibling. I ended up contacting several charities including Cardiac Risk in the Young (CRY) Care For The Family and Think Aorta. All of them were so wonderful and comforting.

CRY arranged a sibling support day, where I connected with two wonderful young women, Sam and Helen, who are my incredible friends to this day. We all share the common though unfortunate experience. We have a void that unites us. I felt like they were the only people in the world to understand what I was going through. We all met in July 2019 and shared experiences of sudden bereavement and the impact on siblings, which is almost always faded into the background, compared to parents' grief. Caring for Families was also another charity I found were there for me, in my desperation.

On social media I connected with grieving siblings. It was my new safe place, knowing id be understood and vice versa.

Saturday 27th July 2019
Went to the sibling support day today at CRY. Met Sam and Helen. Thank you to Alison for connecting us. The circumstances are so sad and heart-breaking. The girls are beautiful. For our brothers x

We formed a WhatsApp group and our emotions and shock overflowed in our messages. We were all on a sinking ship, holding onto each other for support. I don't know what I would've done had I not had this connection to pour out my pain.

Over the coming months I spoke with Claire and Katherine, both siblings in a similar situation. They really helped me too. Thank you so much.

6th August 2019
My heart hurts, so very much. Everyday. Mum said why are you holding him back? Let him continue his journey in peace. It's hard to hear her say that. I'm not holding you back Hermy. I love you. Whilst I'm writing this, the sun is blazing through the window. You're magic!

9th August 2019
Morning until midnight, in my dreams and beyond, you're all I think about. Although it's been this amount of time, I don't feel apart or distant from you. I actually feel very close.

Counselling today was tough. Too many tears Hermy. Then again, my face lights up when I say 'My Hermy'.

15th August 2019
Hermy, it's Rakhi today. Happy Rakhi Hermy. I love you infinitely. More than you'll ever know.

Today was tough. I went into his room. Kneeled at the edge of his bed and just cried, and cried and cried. Rakhi is and always will be a very special event for us both. I would always go and buy him a nice decorated bracelet, with a card and some Indian sweets. It was such a special day for just me and him. For me to bless him with happiness and a long life. I actually brought 12 of the same bracelets in 2019, panic buying so I had lots (of the same design, so I didn't run out) that I'd tied on him the last time… Now I tie them on the teddy bear that's in his room.

*31st **August**: Hermy, I asked mum how she'd describe her life now. She said 'It's very hard, but I have hope.' Isn't that incredible?! That's mummy all over.*

3rd September:

Hermy, I never use words like 'late' or the past tense when it comes to you. You are very much with me. Here. Present. Right by my side. In a new form, but still here. Takes a little adjustment that's all. Until we meet again soon. Love you. Together Forever xxx

4th September

Today I met Jackie, the chaplain at the local hospital. We spoke about you and your closeness and love for the lord. She's wonderful. She said a prayer for us both. Jackie said you are with the lord for eternity. Blessed and loved more. I love that.

Previous to 9th Jan 2019, I used to pray, daily. Saying a prayer of gratitude. Since then, I stopped praying. I had lost faith because I prayed on my knees, in A&E, but no one listened.

Over time, Jackie has grown to be a great friend and real presence in my life. She has brought me back to God. Brought me to Christianity and the love of the lord. I know Hermy loves her too. She's the one who taught me to pray again, to have faith and hope once again. I can't thank her enough. She's really been there for me.

The only thing that gives me some relief is knowing that Hermy knew both mum and I were there, by his side. That would have brought him comfort, even though no one knew what was coming. His last words were 'Let's go home.'

13th September

Had to stay away for a couple of days, with work. Didn't want to leave mum, knowing what state she was in. On the way home in the car, I cried so much and screamed in my car, knowing I wouldn't be heard. H, I can't deal with it. It's so hard. Honestly. Can't live without you. I can't.

15th September

H, it's 15 years since dad passed. I hope he's looking after you. Xx

21ˢᵗ September
Hermy, was talking about you and found a white feather on the wall you sit on. Then, in the garden, mum and I were talking about you and a white butterfly came. You're everywhere. xx

So many things changed and ended, when my beloved went to be with the lord – local Waitrose, his fav progs, etc.

Sunday 13ᵗʰ October – *I pray in his room every Sunday. As I lift the duvet, I can still smell your feet Hermy – now I love that smell. It's so soothing.*

It's funny how the same thing can be so disgusting and so wonderful, depending on the circumstances.

18ᵗʰ Oct – *Tried to exercise but I just I cried and cried and cried...*

I'd written letters about Herman to the Duke of Cambridge, just to share how amazing he is. The Duke of Cambridge acknowledged our love, which was lovely.
I also wrote the Queen a letter about my mum's life

19ᵗʰ Oct – *Mummy got her letter from Her Majesty the Queen! Yes, Queen Elizabeth Hermy! She praised mummy for the life she'd led and mentioned you too!*

20ᵗʰ Oct – *Feels like I'll never be happy again. Everything's changed so much. Nothing will ever be the same. Everything feels so unfair. Bitterly unfair. Feel scared Hermy. I've suffered so much pain, I'm truly exhausted.*

23ʳᵈ Oct – *Hermy, I feel so so so sad. Remember when you said 'if you're sad, I'm sad.'* 😟

*27th **Oct** – Hermy, it's Diwali today. You are the single brightest light in my life. Shine on wherever you are!*

*31st **Oct** – Hermy, sometimes I'm ok… keep my head above water. Then I feel like I'm drowning in my pain – struggling to breathe. I feel so empty. So alone. No one else really gets it. Just you and mummy. Every day we get closer.*

*5th **Nov** – Hermy, mum's been telling me how you come to her – spoken to her many, many times. She hears you speak over her shoulder that you're happy and it's all ok.*

*7th **Nov** – Had a meltdown in my car. Desperate to see you, but don't feel far from you at all.*

*9th **Nov** – I don't know how I get through each day Hermy. This morning I was out in the garden, clearing the leaves. Suddenly a beautiful robin flew over and stood in front of me. It didn't fly away. Instead, hopped around me. My eyes filled up, knowing the robin had brought your spirit close to me, telling me you're right here. Right by my side.*

*12th **Nov** – 05:15am. There was a very bright light and I felt compelled to open the curtain. Infront of me shone a beautiful, perfectly round bright moon. It was right in my view Hermy, as got back into bed. I watched it for 30 mins.*
*   I don't like the word memory…*

21st Nov – Hermy, my heart is forever broken. I will never be the same. It really, really hurts. I just can't believe it… there's a physical pain in my heart.

Your dentist called today, to say your due for a check-up. I couldn't say anything… I just said ok…

24th Nov – Feel like my childhood and future has gone.

'When you lose your parent you lose your past. When you lose a child, you lose your future. When you lose your sibling, you lose your past and future.'

In my opinion, sibling grief has been significantly underrepresented in the world of grief. There's so much focus on parents, spouses and children, but not a lot on siblings. Why not? I struggled to find much, apart from general grief, which can be applied to any relationship. Siblings share the same life growing up. If they're close in age, they share things no one else can. They understand you like no one else. For me, no one else would understand a particular facial expression but him, the jokes, the silences, the chats, singing harmonies together of songs we both enjoy, the giggles and games. You have nicknames for each other that no one else will call you, you speak to each other in funny voices and tones. You have your sibling lingo. No one else gets it or gets you, like your brother or sister. No one.

We were so childish and that continued in our adult lives. Only a few weeks before we reminisced about our childhood and how he was naturally gifted and I had to work hard. I said I was tired of 'finding someone to marry.' So, the plan was for us to grow old together, move to Birmingham and then be in a care home, with our zimmer frames, catching up on the 'good old days.' You've almost got the 'silent authority' to be childish because you can be with your sibling. There's no pressure between you to act mature or grow up. You can be yourself, completely. The conversations you have with them, you don't have with your parents or friends. No one fights like siblings, or loves like siblings. They're supposed to be your one constant throughout life, no matter what. Partners come and go, friends come and go, parents pass on, but your brother and sister are always there. I thought he'd always be with me. I never ever imagined he'd go so soon. We need more awareness and support for bereaved siblings.

Overtime, I experienced so many flashbacks, as soon as I woke up. They played first thing in the morning to last thing at night. Vivid, clear flashbacks of everything – the hospital scene, him lying in a white sheet, mum hitting herself, me visiting him, preparing him and setting him free. These are all embedded in my cortex. Every specific sensory detail such as visual images, smells, sounds and felt experiences are now strongly imprinted and recalled, on an involuntary basis. I have a heightened sensitivity to other sibling relationships and families that consist of more than two. A cold awareness of how cruel life can be. You can't help but say 'Why me? Why us?' It's not helpful to ask such questions, but you ask them anyway and know there are no answers coming back. At the same time, I know how things can change for the better.

I often thought if any of the hospital staff felt guilty in anyway? Do they think about what else they could've done? Do they lose sleep like I do? Or are they that desensitised, having dealt with so many life and death emergencies that they almost become immune? What about the nurse that sent him home with ibuprofen two days before? How does she sleep? How do they feel? I was denied the opportunity to look them in the eye and ask these questions. Apparently, it's not something that is done. I'm still trying to organise a meeting with the trust, but I'm not able to meet with the very people involved at the time. It's absolutely senseless and should be changed, so relatives can gain some comfort.

It is said, the heart undergoes a physical pain and can functionally change due to trauma and psychological impact. I have felt this first hand.

There is no explanation to pain. Nothing will pierce it. It builds up and washes through you.

I was so desperate for something and someone to hold onto, It felt like drowning in an ocean. I remember calling the Samaritans, who were amazing. The guy listening really felt for me, I could tell. I could hear it in his voice when I cried about all the men in my life vanishing and not seeing the family grow. All he could say was 'I'm so sorry' in his helpless attempt to throw something at me

Despite coming from a large extended family, I was disappointed that only a couple of relatives contacted me during my first Rakhi without me being able to physically tie it on him. His birthday. My birthday. They all knew. It hurt because I would have made a real effort if I was on the other side. I would've been aware, emotionally connected to how someone in my position was feeling. Rakhi was very, very difficult. I spent it sobbing.

If I was a friend or relative of someone in my situation, I would've really made an effort to reach out, not just at the point of crisis, but weeks and months afterwards, when the grief really kicks in and starts to take a hold over your life. Apart from a couple of new friends I made and connected with during this journey, no one did. Everyone knew the state of my situation. Yet, only one or two cousins got in touch for his first earth birthday, my first birthday without his physical presence, the first Rakhi. This was all very painful for me, as I would have done more, made arrangements to go out, called, spent time and just thought about the person going through their pain. Thank you to Rashda, Neelam, Helen, Sam, Holly and Jackie. I heard someone say they didn't contact me because they didn't want to remind me. As if I can ever forget. You never forget and don't need 'reminding'. Just goes to show how disconnected people are.

My friend JB who has been incredible in his support during the darkest of times. I'd often call and just breakdown and cry, when I'd be overcome unpredictably at work. Thank you.

You, my friends were there when the world carried on and mine stopped. You were there when the door closed and it was just me and mum. You were there when everyone else went back to their normal routine and I was left picking up the pieces of my shattered world. You kept the light on in my darkness. I'll never forget. Thank you.

December. It was always, always my favourite time of year. My brother's birthday. My birthday. Christmas. Simply magic. Felt like the whole world would be celebrating with us, with lights and joy. I'd always save up my annual leave for December, to enjoy the celebrations in full.

I now dread it. How life and the association of dates and times change. I don't look forward to it. I get nervous and fill with dread, as the month approaches. Now it's like, everyone's still celebrating, but I'm not. That's not right. Not fair.

There were just over four weeks between his earth birthday and angel birthday.

My dear friend Rashda came to the house to celebrate Herman's first 'earth birthday' with me. I did what I always do and spent time decorating, buying his cake and preparing celebrations. Rashda made it even more special, with a beautiful card and sang 'Happy Birthday' with me to him. We cut his favourite cake and I decorated everything as I normally would. I'd always make a big deal out of it and get over excited. He too got excited and I felt he made his presence known, by dropping the memory tree on the floor. It was strange, but I very much felt him there. He always is. That really felt like he was trying to make his presence known! Later I released a golden star-shaped balloon.

To celebrate his angel day, I had to go to church to honour this life. He loves the Lord and that is why it had to be in such a sacred place. It was still within the Xmas period, so there were still decorations, a manger with baby Jesus, beautiful flowers and so much love. There was an air of peace. I had a vision of what I wanted it to be like. My beloved, I know would be blown away. The ceremony consisted of readings by the priest about love and the moment when Martha said to Jesus, 'If you came, my brother would still be here. Jesus replied, your brother is alive and has risen.' I love this so much. His favourite songs – Mariah Carey, 'Joy to the World', 'Silent Night' and 'Vison of Love' were played. To have those songs played in his name, in St Philips Cathedral on his angel day, was such a blessing. I could see his wide smile.

9ᵗʰ Jan 2020. My speech:

Today is Herman's angel birthday. God's plan was underway for Herman to be with his lord Jesus Christ. The smile in his photo shows just how happy he is to be an angel. Herman loves the lord. The first thing he would say is 'Glory to God.' Christ is Lord. He found solace in the Lord from what was a tumultuous life. Lost in a world he couldn't navigate. A tortured genius and child prodigy, unable to bear the burden of his exceptional abilities and expectations. It was in Christ he sought refuge and found love. Days before he went to be with the lord, the last pages of his bible read 'I pray to you O Lord. In the time of your favour. In your great love, answer me, with your sure salvation. In your great mercy turn to me. Hasten to lord to save me.' It is because of his great love for the Lord was so powerful his silent cries for peace were heard and Christ took him under his wings. Although today marks a measured 12 months since he become an angel I don't feel any distance from him at all. He's still very much with me. He's still very much a fundamental part of my life. I believe we are not our physical bodies. We are energy and love. He is right here carrying me through the dense fog of grief.

9ᵗʰ Jan was still the Christmas period and God prepared Herman for his homecoming. For us it was sudden and our heart was ripped out. For Herman it was quick transition to heaven. His last words were let's go home. I know that's where he is – at peace, with Christ. Herman, I love you more than you can imagine. I can't wait to be with you again – it's just a matter of time. See you soon. Thank you to each of you, for being here today, but also for supporting me over last 12 months. Your love and kindness has protected me when I felt so alone. You showed compassion and understanding without judgement. Thank you. Listening to me, sitting in silence or just showing me you care. It would bring great comfort to Herman too, knowing there are angels on earth.

Thank you so much to my friends and family who came with me in support of this very special moment. You are not forgotten.

The impact of something so horrendous is a glaze over everything in my life now. Once a compassionate human, full of empathy, I suddenly found myself void of any feelings. I didn't feel anything for anyone anymore. I simply could not care. I don't know if it was because I had exhausted every emotion in me that I had nothing left or that my heart had just turned into a stone – empty of blood and or heartbeat. Cold. Hard. Colourless and pulseless.

When people talk to me about their son or brother, who's the same age as our beloved, it's hard not to think about how life might have turned out – his children. My nieces and nephews. Mum as a grandma. It's' a loud reminder of what we don't have and what could have been. Everything now has a sting in it. An ache in reflection. I remember someone said life just isn't fair. Isn't that so hard to accept? It's a very natural response to our story.

I asked mum if she thinks she's strong. Her answer was 'Yes. But, before I am strong, I am a mother.' Wow. I understand all mothers have a unique bond and level of affection for their child but I don't see many with the intensity and consistency of devotion as my mother. She recently told me she was never very maternal, when she was younger or the type of woman that always knew she wanted to have kids. However, once nature took its course and she had us, it became a love that killed her and forced her to live at the same time. Despite enduring a severed physical connection with one child, she has her heart beating for another. I guess that is the power of a mother. I cannot yet understand this feeling. Hopefully, one day I will.

The impact of what happened to him, continues on us.

May 2020
Went to Waitrose. Mum was having a nap when I left to go shopping. I knew her phone was with her. At Waitrose I tried calling her and she didn't pick up. I tried again and again and again. I remember thinking the phone was next to her, so why isn't she picking up?!! I freaked out and thought she had

died! I thought she'd gone into a diabetic coma and passed in her sleep. My heart was racing, I was in full blown panic mode. Rushed to the car and drove home, dreading what I would discover...
She was ok.

My mind is constantly on high alert. Therefore, the precognitive circuit is activated reducing the likelihood that I am engaging the prefrontal cortex.

July 2020
Mum's been screaming in the middle of the night. I have to wake up and make sure she's ok.

Some days are lighter than others. I'm not the same person, so how can my life be the same as it used to be? Joy has just developed a new skin. It's very sensitive.

Herman and Ramen are always one. Together. There is no Ramen without Herman. This is why I feel like I'm the one that's lost. Part of Ramen has vanished. Dissolved with my grief. The jokes, the giggles, the expressions that only me and my brother would get. No one else does. They never will. The plans that we'd made about growing old together.

Initially, when this tragedy happened, Herman became (or should I say became even more) of an obsession. I couldn't stop looking at his photos and videos, talking to him, making him a part of all that I do. Now, in 2021, I cannot look at any photos or videos. Once in a while if I'm craving to hear his voice, I will only listen not watch. It's interesting how that response has evolved over time. Now looking at his photo feels like touching a severed nerve or an open wound. Perhaps this will again change over time. I'm glad I have so many videos and photos with him. They are now too precious.

Looking back now, what's interesting is how God knew Herman's time was limited and we packed so much in together as a family. Now it feels like it was a race against time. Between

2017 and 2019 we travelled to seven countries, saw his favourite singers in concert, went out for lots of lovely meals, expressed so much love and talked about death. Now it all makes sense. All the pieces fit together. We just didn't know what was coming…

My brother was in a great place and we shared so much love and joy. Then, God took him home. Sigh. Life for him had come full circle. Herman's last words were actually 'let's go home'…

I'm not here to say get through or recover from your grief, because the truth is, for me I will never. I have to learn to carry it with me daily, because it's always a presence in my life. Instead of it being dull and black and white, I can start to add a little colour to brighten things up a touch – maybe add a smile, roll my eyes like him, laugh at what he would laugh at make comments that he would make in certain situations. This just makes the load a little lighter to carry.

Ever since my world fell apart with this event, the question 'How are you?' now feels like one of the most difficult questions to answer…

There was no way that I would be in the house during Xmas of 2019. So, we booked to go away. It wasn't the best break, because our emotions were still so raw but we went.

What's next.....

'What is stronger than the human heart which shatters over and over and still lives.'

Rupi Kaur

3/1/2020

Got back from Morocco. Mum kept saying 'Why can't you be normal?' What is normal? I will never be normal or the same again.

Can't help but think about the lead up to the events that unfolded only 12 months earlier.

8th Jan – The lights have been left on all night.

9th Jan – Happy angel Birthday Hermy! I love you more than you can ever imagine. You had a very, very magical day today. Very magical.

I thought I'd feel low and extremely distraught. However, I actually felt lifted by a greater force. I know it was God. He had me in the palm of his hand.

I had enlarged a photo of my beloved, which was placed in the cathedral. There you were as a big angel – so happy and delighted in the Lord's house, surrounded by the nativity.

After the initial tribute, 'Silent Night' by Mariah Carey was played. It was so beautiful. This was followed by my tribute and then your favourite song Hermy – 'Vision of Love' by Mariah Carey!

Later in the evening, mum and I went to feed 100 homeless people, in his name. I'd ordered a beautiful white heavenly cake, which read 'Love from Herman'. I told everyone it was his special angel birthday.

10th Jan 2020
Mum and I argued tonight. Sometimes the enormity of our pain spills into attacking one another, unable to cope with the force of destruction in our lives. Our heart, ripped out just like that. We both feel so alone, drowning in our pain. We cannot save each other.

10:45pm – I've noticed a part of me is comfortable in pain. It's a familiar place, because I've been surrounded by so much of it all my life.

11th Jan – 07:45am. Mum crawls into bed with me. She always does after we argue. She says we are both hurting. She just gets it, without me saying anything. It's the same with Hermy. Every time she would think of him, when he wasn't at home, the doorbell would ring and he'd be there. The energy between us is incredible. It's still there, beyond our physical presence.

12th Jan 2020
I'm dying every day. Not living anymore Hermy. Going through the motions of what is necessary. Every day, I feel like I don't want to be here. Life is so cruel. So unfair. Why do some people have it all and others have nothing?

Where are you now Hermy? Are you having a magical experience?

I've been in bed ALL day. Woke up at 4pm! Mum came into my room a few times for cuddles. She said no matter how old I get, she will keep being there, giving advice, telling me off, making up and being mum forever. I said 'I want you to hate me.' She said this is something that is impossible because I am a part of her.

Travelling is a passion. Always has been since I could afford to. Moreover, I enjoy travelling with myself. Many people are uncomfortable being alone or spending time with themselves. I find it therapeutic, as I get to rediscover myself, in so many new ways. It helps me understand myself so much and in ways in which I've adapted to change and what I've learnt.

Following months of despair and sadness, I arranged to go. After some self-debate on whether I should go to Africa or South America for my retreat, I decided on Africa. The raw nature, authenticity and an unknown appealed to me. Africa it is.

After 2019, I wanted to escape everything. I knew I coudnt escape my mind, but knew Africa would bring new perspectives, a refreshed focus and reflection.

15th Jan
Last few days I've been packing for my trip to South Africa. I need to do it for me. With me. To rediscover the new Ramen and travel into the unknown fearlessly.

Jan 18th 2020
1:30am. Opened the curtains. There you are, filling the dark blue sky, with the brightest, clearest sparkling stars. I haven't seen anything like it in a long time.

Getting ready to leave. I hear you say 'What about mummy?' We are never apart. She's not just strong. She's a rock.

Long flight to Cape Town. Not sure how I feel. Scared. Anxious. Nervous. Excited. Fearless and ok all at the same time.

On the flight. I looked through the window of various shades of blue, pink and orange skies and sunsets, the clouds, the vast African landscape. Saw you everywhere but found you nowhere. Listened to songs, cried alone to one side so I wouldn't be seen.

You're all I think about.

Flying over the vast landscape of Africa, and rising above the clouds, I searched for my Hermy, with tears in my eyes I leaned against the window seat, with tears streaming down my face, I tried not to show nearby passengers.

It was a time for me to spend time with myself and process what the hell had happened over the past 12 months. How have I moved through this mess? How did I travel on my own to Africa, given I had experienced so much the past few months?

19th Jan
Checked into the hotel. Absolutely exhausted.

20th Jan – Went to Robben Island today and absorbed the history of Nelson Mandela's life and a view from his prison cell.

The trip is absolutely amazing. I love Africa. It's what everyone says it is like. Just having the open space, I felt like I could breathe. One of the highlights amongst many was riding a very rusty bicycle through the open, rolling streets of Soweto. It was one of those simple life pleasures.

22nd – Took a flight to Johannesburg and a cycle ride on the streets of Soweto. It was the simplicity of riding a bicycle, which wasn't the best quality, a bit rusty and cranky but I just cycled through endless roads in beautiful Soweto, surrounded by white butterflies. I absolutely loved it!

Later, I got to my lodge. My room key – number 5 (his earth day). Hermy, you are everywhere!!

24th Jan – I'm in Kruger National Park Hermy! On a safari. Beautiful. I'm shattered.

28th Jan – In Zimbabwe. Next stopover is called 'Hermitz'. 😁😁😁😁. There are white butterflies everywhere!

One evening, we were given the opportunity to experience the African sky at night, in the greater Kruger area. The sky was perfectly pure. I stood there and witnessed the most vivid, beautiful starlit sky. There was one star that was the brightest. I stood under it, my eyes filled up. It was dark, so no one could see my tears rolling down my face. Previously, when I asked Hermy where I'd find him, he said, 'In the stars.' The brightest star was in my gaze. I knew, as silent tears rolled down my face it was my beloved.

Later that evening, they turned the lights off and told us to look up at the sky. It was full of the most amazing stars. It just so happens that I was standing under the brightest star! Tears strolled down my cheeks. I connected. It was so profound.

Hermy was everywhere. I felt is presence and still do. Another highlight was standing on the top of Table Mountain, where the clouds were so close, I felt I was close to heaven. Close to my beloved.

21ˢᵗ - Table Mountain. Once at the top, Hermy I felt the closest I have ever felt to heaven. I was actually in a cloud. It was so magical. I surrendered, manifested and built faith all at once.

We also travelled to Mpumalanga, to see God's window. It all felt so wonderful to feel so close to God and the heavens. So close to my beloved brother.

31ˢᵗ Jan 2020
Toady we travelled to Victoria Falls for the final night of my tour.

I had set my intention to face any fear. The fear was the bungee jump, off Victoria falls bridge. I thought about it a lot and knew I could do it. This time I felt fearless. I looked fear in the face and did it. I felt like nothing could be worse than what had already happened, so bring it on.

As my turn approached, I got strapped up and harnessed up securely. With only towels holding my legs together and some straps, I was slowly led to the foot of the bridge. My hands are in tight fists, as the fear builds up throughout my body. The two guys either side of me forced my hands to open. I had to, reluctantly.
'You are my single, constant focus Hermy.' I'm scared, nervous, sweaty, heart is pounding. They say, 'Come forward – a little more, as they perch my feet on the edge of the bridge. A little more, more... then... 5,4,3,2,1...' Hermyyyyyyyyyy!!
The initial drop was the worst – the scariest. Then I tumbled upside down, dangling like a tittle fish on the end of a rod. I bounced and swung and floated. It was the most incredible experience. 111ft jump.
When I was on the edge, I closed my eyes and just thought of you. It was all about you.
I did it Hermy I did it!

I don't feel pain anymore, because my 'worldview' of pain has changed. Like I've been on the extreme end of this spectrum. This is my tsunami. Suddenly everything else that used to bother me no longer touches me. That's all now a drop in the ocean. However, I now live in this opposing mental world where on one side I have peace that he is in peace, then the stark contrast of another, where the passing of time is making me uncomfortable, because I'm so desperate to see him as the longing grows and I still have bouts of shock. At the same time I feel his presence in all that I do.

Having observed how people are so conditioned by society, it's made me realise how much I don't like to conform. Instead, I'm curious about everything. Even when it came to this book. Whilst researching how to write and get published, 'experts' said 'Make sure it has an ending, 'What can be learnt?' etc., etc. The point is that there is no ending because we are constantly evolving, learning and developing. I'm continuing on this life journey to discover what happens next?

One thing I know for sure is that nothing stays the same forever. We'll evolve with our circumstances and relationships. Life will continually teach us. Transform us until we become the best of ourselves. I'm not focused on the future. I've learned to be even more present. Sometimes it's ok to stay in bed and wallow in self-pity. We're always told to 'learn and grow.' Sometimes you just don't have the energy to do that and you want to sit and sulk. That's ok. Just don't do it forever. This book is about love, grief, siblings, forgiveness, breaking the mould, rising again and carrying hope in your pocket at all times. I have started to pray again, after over one year. I have since felt the Lord's protection and grace over me.

I've kept my brother central to all that I do. I brought a house and named it after him. His affectionate home name is Honey. In the garden, got a sign made 'Honey's Garden', a bird tree that says 'Love from Honey'. He is in everything that I do. I feel scared of all the time that will pass between us, in the physical sense, but I'm hoping we've had more time on this earth than we have apart and it is only a matter of time before we meet again. At the same time I feel his energy abundantly and no distance between us. My emotional landscape comprises of an amalgamation of opposing and contradicting sensations.

Even as I sit and write this, I think about all those who suffer profound grief, but carry on living somehow, someway. They may not have the energy to write a book or anything that takes a lot of work, but they put one foot in front of another and carry on, the best way they know how, still continuing to make a difference in their world. They carry a burden and void that no-one can see and it surfaces when triggered. Grief alone is totally exhausting. It obliterates your energy. I'm 33 months in right now, and bit by bit I'm trying with whatever reserve I have left from my day, to write. Death is coming to us all. We need to be more comfortable talking about it. Not shutting it away, like it's a taboo topic or be fearful about it. Let's embrace it and talk to our loved ones about it. It will help us live better. I'm so glad I did with my Hermy. There was no need to, because he was well. I just felt it in my heart. Now I know the conversation was meant for a reason.

What and where would people be, had what happened to them, not happened? We all have a story. I wish those with immense talent are given an opportunity to make their mark, no matter what their struggle. I've seen so many families destroyed because of mental health, dysfunction and aggression. All I have to say is, had I not looked beyond all these factors, I would never have had the opportunity to love and spend precious time with my beloved as much as we did. A lot of forgiveness took place and love was restored. Holding onto anger would not have enabled this to take place.

Journal: Sat 23rd June 2007 – last night mummy and I had a little fall out. I had a little me time, slept peacefully and prayed. This morning I woke to find a beautiful rose plant mummy brought for me and put in my room to cheer me up. What a wonderful loving gesture.

My mum is the most incredible lady. When she lives in a world and a culture full of comparison and judgement, she always sees hope. In her darkest moments she sees light. When the world talks about me being a single Indian girl in my 40s, she says, 'Life can change at any time.' – for the good, not just the bad. We don't know who you'll meet and how great your life will be.' Even now, my mum kisses and cuddles me. When I come down the stairs, she'll be singing a loving Indian song. First thing in the morning we have a cuddle. I know she is my saving grace on earth. Her affection is so loud and expressive. That's mum all over. I love her beyond measure. Despite her difficulties, she never wants sympathy from anyone. She doesn't want anyone to ever feel sorry for her. She actually hates it. I hear so many comments from people that know mum before she got married saying, 'You've been so unlucky, or you've had a terrible life' etc. Whilst she listens, she does not accept that narrative for her life. Nor do I. This is a woman, like millions of others, who travelled to a foreign country to marry a man she never knew to make a life. Although her husband didn't work, she did. She made an effort to upskill herself, find work and learn how to drive. To become independent. She raised two beautiful children and showered them with so much love. Love that will last several lifetimes. Her expression of her love is boundless. I don't know many Indian mothers, of that generation that kiss, cuddle and sing to their children. Our pictures together express that unbounding love in abundance. We don't have photos where we're just standing like statues next to one another. Our photos are filled with tight squeezes and bursts of affection.

Saturday 11th April 2004
Today, me, Hermy and mummy sat down with a mug of Horlicks each and had a heart to heart. A few tears were shed too. Mummy said we are her priority and she shared some life lessons. This mother truly loves her children and wants us to know. It was wonderful to listen to her. She really speaks from the heart. There is never any doubt in our mind.

Friends often wonder why I'm so close to my mum. I go everywhere with her, take her to spas and holidays, etc. It's simply because she is the most open, honest and chilled person who knows me inside out. I can talk to her better than friends and she understands me like no other. She knows about the guys in my life and will always give me the best advice. There are times I don't say anything and she just knows because she paid attention. She feels. Deeply. She's not just maternal, she's a natural.

Her life has always been about others – be it her children, family, friends and strangers. Sure, she's dealt with adversity. Who hasn't? For her, the worst being her first born child take his last breadth right in front of her. She describes it as the worst pain of her life. An indescribable internal pain, that eats away all the time. When people say 'you're so strong', mum's response is always to say it's her pain, so she has to own it. It's not for the display of others. What people see and what she feels are 2 very different faces. The way she deals with it is by knowing unfortunately, she is not alone. She said this will happen to us all, but her pain comes from the unnatural sequence of the child passing before the parent. That's what hurts the most. 'He shouldn't have gone before me,' she says. Mum has started to pray again and asks God for strength to deal with and carry this heavy intolerable suffering. She seeks peace. Her approach to life is to look at people who suffer more than her. 'There are people much worse off' she says. It's a sort of self-help mechanism, to save one from drowning in their own pain.

My mum has travelled the world with her children. Whilst she may not have had love from a husband, she wasn't void of love altogether. She indulged in it, with her children. Her attitude is always, 'I am independent, had a good life, good job' and the one thing that's most important to her is her self-respect. That is something she had earned and it cannot be taken away by anyone. Every day she amazes me.

So far, I have had counselling, been on antidepressants, been to the depths of my despair but also lived on the edge of life, by facing a fear – travelled alone to find me again, jumped 111ft off Victoria Falls, brought a new house and a new puppy. I've written a book and got it published. I've put my life out there to help anyone that feels like they cannot carry on. I've designed and helped to create a website, specifically for bereaved siblings, so those experiencing the pain that I do, don't feel so alone just like I did. Through my tragedy I've pushed through to do something that matters to me and will help others. I found focus through pain and pushed through to make it happen. It's taken me years. It's not easy. There were times I wanted to go to sleep and not wake up. But, I've been kind to myself, taken one day at a time, as and when I've wanted to do anything I have. I haven't forced myself. As and when it felt right for me I did it. This is the result. No one day is the same. Each day brings its own challenges. It took me four months to write this book because I had so much to say and it has been very cathartic for me. I hope this book touches you too, in some way you connect and know that you have it in you to get through each day, by being kind to yourself when trying to cope with the challenges and changes life brought you whatever challenge it is you are facing.

2 Corinthians 4:16 NLT

That is why we never give up. Though our bodies are dying, our spirits are being renewed every day.

I don't know what the future will hold, all I have now is hope in my pocket. I now have a yearning for life and death. Death is a new baseline. An extreme baseline, which offers a new perspective on issues that would previously bother me. This is not the end but a desire for an understanding of what life is all about and what happens next. If anything, it feels like this is just the beginning. I hope this life becomes my testimony, that this too shall pass and all will be well, in the end.

I love looking through my journals and reading the simple moments that were captured.

1ˢᵗ May 2012
Me and Hermy spoke. He said 'Think about the good things in your life.'

Now, that is what I will do. He told me if I'm sad then he's sad, so I will try not to be that anymore.

My life so far will not define my entire life. Who knows what's in store for me and you reading?

All I know is that if I can navigate this seismic event and see hope through the dense fog of grief then nothing else can affect me. I'm not shy to say I am so proud of myself for writing a book and getting it published! My first book. Through the pain, I found power. I pushed forward and created this book. Gods grace surrounded me throughout the journey and my mum is just magic that keeps me going. In my eulogy, I promised my beloved brother that I would continue to make him proud. I hope I have achieved some of this with writing this book – our book. I will continue to do what I can in his name. I can see him smiling with pride at his little sister. It's always about my Hermy!

They say the brightest stars shine in the darkest sky's... let's see.

Thank you for reading my story.

Love,

Herman's sister xx

www.ingramcontent.com/pod-product-compliance
Lightning Source LLC
Chambersburg PA
CBHW031630040426
42452CB00007B/759